I10668258

People
Parables

242
C 323

People Parables

James E. Carter

BAKER BOOK HOUSE
Grand Rapids, Michigan

Copyright © 1973 by
Baker Book House Company

ISBN: 0-8010-2348-3

Second printing, June 1981

PHOTOLITHOPRINTED BY CUSHING - MALLOY, INC.
ANN ARBOR, MICHIGAN, UNITED STATES OF AMERICA

For
Carole

459

preface

From the most common things can come significant teachings. From the everyday, the common, or the usual we can learn important truths about God, our world, and ourselves.

The earliest definition for a parable that I learned is "a parable is an earthly story with a heavenly meaning."

These are earthly stories. They have been suggested by the sayings, the experiences, and the foibles of earthly people. From them we can derive heavenly meanings.

They were first written for the weekly paper of the First Baptist Church, Natchitoches, Louisiana. Some of them have been reprinted by the *Baptist Message*, the Baptist Bulletin Service, *Home Life, Church Administration, Proclaim,* and the Stewardship Commission of the Southern Baptist Convention, and in my earlier book, *A Sourcebook for Stewardship Sermons.*

Several secretaries have typed them in their present form. Particularly, Mrs. Ola Clinton and Mrs. Carolyn Lee have been helpful. For their help I am grateful.

And, of course, I am grateful to the people of the First Baptist Church who first received them and to my children, Craig, Keith, and Chyrisse, who inspired many of them.

Jesus spoke in parables and the people heard Him gladly. I trust He can still speak to people through these people parables.

James E. Carter
Pastor's Study
First Baptist Church
Natchitoches, Louisiana

Contents

part one

ABOUT
CHRISTIAN
SALVATION

forgiveness:
human and divine

Not long ago a father brought his son into the pastor's office to talk about becoming a Christian. (This is most commendable and it would be well if more fathers took such an interest in the spiritual welfare of their children.)

In the course of the discussion, the pastor sought to establish the relationship between repentance and forgiveness. He thought he would make the point by referring to an incident that could happen in his own life.

"What would happen," asked the pastor, "if you broke a plate of your mother's china, and then you told her that you were really and truly sorry that you had done it?" His answer was quick as a flash. "She would say, 'That doesn't make a bit of difference; the plate is still broken!'"

Art Linkletter has made a fortune from recording the wise and cute sayings of children. This child's answer was more than cute. It helped to point up the difference between human forgiveness and divine forgiveness.

Often we humans think more of the act that has been performed. Even being sorry afterwards doesn't really make too much difference to us. The deed is committed and the harm is done. But God looks at the heart. When we are truly sorry (repentant), He forgives us and restores us to a right relationship with Himself. That's the difference between human forgiveness and God's forgiveness. But then, that's the difference between people and God.

how to be a church member
without being committed

There is an interesting little book of satire entitled *How to Become a Bishop Without Being Religious*. The thesis of this book is that to get ahead in the ministry one doesn't have to really *be* religious; he just has to *look* pious.

Interestingly enough, this is old hat. Church people have been doing it for years. Any number of ways have been devised to indicate church membership and church involvement without really being committed to Christ, the Head of the church.

Some do it with their presence. They make sure that they are at the church for everything. But sometimes this very activism hides real confrontation with the Lord. They often are too busy for a devotional life.

Some do it with their payments. Being generous in gifts to the church is considered by many to cover a multitude of sins. Some people have even been known to tithe thinking that this excused them from any other obligation to Christ or the church.

Some do it with their pretense. The book referred to above mentions the "stained glass voice." We have learned certain facial expressions, certain phrases, and certain postures that seem to indicate real piosity. But often these are pretense. Underneath, the person still has a heart untouched and a spirit unmoved.

What do we need? Jesus called it the "new birth." This indicates a change so radical that it is like being born anew. What the Lord demands of us is real commitment—giving our lives to Him completely and unreservedly in faith. Elton Trueblood says the church ought to be the "company of the committed." Until it truly is, many people still will want to know how to be a church member without being committed. But God wants from us both confession and commitment.

the source of tranquility
and the
sea of tranquility

Boy! Would you ever have believed it? Even after seeing it on television it was still hard to believe. The whole nation was thrilled and recharged with pride and the sense of accomplishment because the first men on the moon were Americans. The marvels of modern technology allowed us to participate in this historic occasion in ways different from all other great events of history. We actually felt vitally involved in the whole project.

But what will it mean? Howard K. Smith, the television news commentator, said, "The greatest benefit may be spiritual." Then he read a quotation from Morison and Commager's basic American history textbook on the effect of the discovery of America on Europe.

But spirituality goes farther than just an uplifting of the national spirit. To be truly spiritual also means that it will bring us closer to God and to His purpose for the life of mankind.

For the most part, the astronauts are men of faith. That in itself has had a tremendous spiritual effect on our country. Buzz Aldrin took a part of the communion loaf from his church with him to the moon. There, in one of his rest periods, he ate it, symbolically joining the other members of his home church in worship.

The exploration of space has been promoted for peaceful purposes. The inscription of the plaque left on the moon reads, "Here men from the planet earth first set foot on the moon July 1969 A.D. We came in peace for all mankind."

When President Nixon spoke by telephone to astronauts Armstrong and Aldrin, he said, "As you talk to us from the Sea of Tranquility, it inspires us to redouble our efforts to bring tranquility to man."

And it does! We who are Christians know that true tranquility for men comes only through faith in Jesus Christ and commitment to Him. Even on the moon, tranquility is found through Christ. Let us pray that as men now have walked on the Sea of Tranquility, more of us will know the source of tranquility—Jesus, the Christ.

taking the risk
out of dying

Not long ago a newspaper carried an unusual head-line. It read, "Test Takes Risk Out of Dyeing." Of course it was talking about dyeing hair. The expert on feminine beauty who was being quoted said that a woman should make a strand test on her hair before dyeing all of it. That makes sense. But it was the headline that attracted atten-tion. Undoubtedly it directed the thoughts of some read-ers far beyond dyeing hair.

The risk was taken out of dying long ago. Jesus took the risk out of dying. When He died on the cross for our sins and then rose again by the power of God, He took all the risk out of dying. Jesus defeated death.

The Bible assures us that the Christian also can defeat death through Christ. The resurrection of Jesus from the dead is spoken of as the "firstfruits"—the promise that those who are united by faith to Christ also will defeat death.

Defeating death does not mean that we will not die. We are human and mortal. But defeating death does mean that we will not be defeated by it. Death is an end but it is not the end. God has promised us eternal life. The future of the Christian is not annihilation, or oblivion, or eternal death. We do not have to fear death because we know that God will go through this experience with us just as He has been with us through every other experience.

The risk was taken out of dying long ago. Jesus did it

through the cross and the resurrection. We can experience this assurance by faith in Christ.

just who is
a disciple?

Chyrisse had just made her public profession of faith and was baptized into church membership. The Lord's Supper service on Easter evening would be the first Lord's Supper service in which she could participate.

This became the subject of discussion at the dinner table. She said, "Daddy, what will I do if I start to take it and one of the disciples shakes his head?"

Well, we usually call them deacons. But, no doubt disciples is a good word for them, too.

Who is a disciple, anyway? We usually define *disciple* too narrowly. When the word is mentioned we usually think of the twelve apostles, the first disciples of Jesus.

Actually, *disciple* is not just a religious word. My dictionary indicates that it means anyone who receives instructions from another. So a disciple can be someone other than a religious disciple.

A disciple of Jesus Christ, then, is one who learns from Jesus Christ; he is a person who takes instructions from Jesus.

All true deacons are also disciples. In fact, all of the rest of us are disciples, too.

Discipleship is basic to the Christian faith. It is not reserved for a select few. It is the response that all of us make to Jesus. It is following Him, learning from Him, obeying Him, and seeking to live like Him.

The New Testament gives several marks of discipleship. Discipleship involves such things as faith, obedience, trust, love, and hope. All of these must be centered in Christ.

The first disciples were those persons who recognized Jesus as the Savior and committed their lives to Him.

They lived with Him, stayed close to Him, learned from Him, and were obedient to Him. Present disciples must do the same.

Just who is a disciple? Anyone who follows Christ in faith, love, and obedience, is His disciple.

a definition
of faith

Grandfather Carter was past eighty when he took his first airplane ride. He had been visiting one of his daughters who lived in Kansas City, Missouri, and then from there he flew to Indianapolis, Indiana, to visit another daughter. When he got back home he was eager to tell his son about the trip.

"Son," he said, "I didn't put my full weight down on that seat the whole trip."

Now, that is not faith.

Putting your full weight on God is faith. Faith is trusting God without any holding back, without any restraint, and without any reservations.

Many of us practice faith the same way Grandfather Carter rode the airplane. We don't really put our full weight down.

For instance, we may give God our problems through prayer—and still worry about them.

We may turn a situation over to God—and still try to manipulate the outcome.

We may say that we trust God's own Word—and still try to second guess the outcome.

We may accept a promise of God—and still try to bring about the result ourselves.

We may say that we accept Christ by faith for salvation—and still try to work our way to heaven.

That is not faith. Faith is belief; it is trust; it is commitment. Faith is giving ourselves completely to God; putting our full weight on Him.

the cost of peace
with God

Some time ago, the First Baptist Church in Shreveport, Louisiana, received the following letter. Enclosed in the letter was a nickel. The letter read:

> During the last few years the Baptist Tea Room was open, I lived in Shreveport and ate there regularly. The food was delicious. There was one time the lady cashier gave me 5 cents change too much and I knew it, knowing all the time I was doing wrong. I am sending it to you today so that I can have peace with God about this.
>
> Your friend in Christ,

How much does it cost to have peace with God?

Apparently, for this individual, peace with God cost just a nickel.

Over the years this dishonesty had bothered him and weighed heavily on his conscience. With the return of the money, the conviction was relieved, his conscience was clear, and he had peace with God.

Usually it takes more than that to clear a conscience and to ease conviction. But a nickel's worth is a start. And we all should make the start.

What does it cost you to have peace with God? It cost Jesus His life. Listen to the Scriptures:

"For Christ himself has brought us peace. . . . So Christ came and preached the Good News of peace to all—to you Gentiles, who were far away from God, and to the Jews, who were near to him. It is through Christ that all of us, Jews and Gentiles, are able to come in the one spirit into the presence of the Father" (Eph. 2:14, 17-18 TEV).

"Now that we have been put right with God through faith, we have peace with God through our Lord Jesus Christ" (Rom. 5:1 TEV).

To be put right with God you must accept Christ as Savior, who has provided peace by His death on the cross. Peace with God costs a whole lot. It cost Christ His life. It costs you the commitment of your life to Christ.

a case of mistaken
identity . . . and a goal

A local pastor was asked to give the benediction for the summer commencement exercises at a large university. While they were lined up waiting to march in, a friend came by with his little son. Upon seeing the pastor in the line, the boy said, "Look, Daddy, there's Mr. Jesus."

Of course it was a case of mistaken identity.

But then every Christian should try to make his life as much as possible like the life of Christ. Kagawa, the great Japanese Christian servant, used to say that the goal of evangelism was to have a whole world of "little Christs."

In the New Testament we keep running across disquieting phrases like "be ye transformed . . ."; "we are his workmanship created in Christ Jesus . . ."; "to be conformed to the image of his son . . ."; and "Be ye therefore perfect, even as your Father which is in heaven is perfect."

The goal of the Christian is Christlikeness. We are to pattern our lives after His life. We are to use Him for our only standard of judgment. We can never be satisfied with ourselves until we measure up to the Lord Himself.

"Mr. Jesus" will not be seen walking our streets or standing around in our hallways. But each of us can seek to reach God's goal for our lives until we mirror the character of the Savior. Wouldn't it be great if one of us were so successful in this endeavor that he could be called "Mr. Jesus"?

a picture
of atonement

When I was nine years old I joined the YMCA for the summer. One of my friends who lived near me would go with me three days a week to the "Y" to play and swim. Each time we went, we were given enough money to ride the bus to the trolly and then to town and back home again.

One day my friend's mother gave him an extra dime so that we could buy a treat after we were dismissed. To us, it seemed that the session would never end. After we had finished swimming and were dressed, we rushed to the corner Walgreen drugstore. We mounted the stools at the lunch counter in that cool, air-conditioned store, ready to order. Then we saw behind the counter the mouth-watering pictures depicting the various choices for food and drinks.

One item really caught our eyes—a chocolate ice-cream soda. Neither of us had ever tried one before. And we gave no thought to the cost. If there ever was a case of "over-sell," this was it. So we each ordered one.

I never tasted anything so good. Then the waitress brought our ticket. We looked at it, and nearly died. It was for fifty cents and all we had was a dime. I could just see myself washing dishes all night long. We didn't know what to do.

Just when we had sunk to our lowest, a man who had been flirting with the waitress reached between us, picked up the ticket, and said, "That's all right, boys, I'll take care of it." This benefactor, whom we had never seen before, paid our debt and rescued us.

This is what Christ did for us on the cross. We had a valid debt to pay because of our sin. But Christ took it Himself. He blotted it out. He nailed it to the cross. We have been rescued and forgiven. Our relationship with God has been restored.

a subtle cross

The president of Laukhuff Stained Glass Company of Memphis, Tennessee, was at the church to measure for the stained glass windows which were to go over and on each side of the baptistry. While she and the pastor were waiting for the contractor to arrive, they discussed possible designs for the windows.

When they started talking about the two side windows, she asked, "Would you object if I put a subtle cross in each of those windows?" She was assured that this would be fine.

What do you think about the remark? Do you have a subtle cross? How do you go about getting crucified subtly? When Jesus asked us to take up our cross and follow Him, did He mean for us to take up a subtle cross?

There was nothing subtle about the cross on which Christ died. It was set up on the "place of the skull" publicly. Everyone knew that a crucifixion was underway. The place was so cosmopolitan that they had to write the sign in three languages.

Christ doesn't mean for us to take up a subtle cross either. He calls us to boldly declare ourselves to Him, to openly accept Him, and to actually surrender ourselves to Him.

A subtle cross would be a bloodless cross. And Christ would not allow that. A subtle cross would be a cross without commitment. There is no place in the Christian faith for that. A subtle cross would be a silent, secret cross. But faith demands open expression.

Too many of us have tried a subtle cross too long. Let's follow Christ's call and take up the cross of self-surrender and full commitment and follow Him—all the way.

enough of calvary

The tourists had just walked from the Garden Tomb

to Gordon's Calvary. The Garden Tomb is one of the two spots in Jerusalem thought to be the burial place of Jesus. The other spot is inside the walls of the Old City. It is marked by an old church known as the Church of the Holy Sepulchre, which is shared by six Christian denominations.

The Garden Tomb was discovered about the turn of the century. It is outside the city walls, as was the tomb where Jesus was laid. It is carved out of solid rock with a groove for a stone wheel to be rolled to shut the entrance. Its setting is a beautiful little garden. If it is not the actual tomb where Jesus was laid, it is much like it.

Gordon's Calvary is right next to the Garden Tomb. It is indeed a skull-shaped hill. Presently, there is a Moslem cemetery on top of it.

From a spot next to the garden you can see the shape of the skull. Many people were taking pictures of it. They would stand next to the sign with Calvary in the background. One man was heard to say to another, "Jimmy, do you want me to take some pictures for you?" The other replied, "No, I've got enough of Calvary."

Haven't we all got enough of Calvary?

Calvary means death. It calls for the death of self and the death of our ambitions and the death of our self-seeking.

Calvary calls for a sacrifice. You cannot think of your relationship to Calvary without realizing that Christ has called you to self-sacrifice.

Jesus went to Calvary for us. He took upon Himself our sins and died in self-sacrifice for us.

Jesus calls us to Calvary. When He told us to take up our cross and follow Him, that is what He meant. A cross always meant death. Paul said, "I am crucified with Christ." And we must be identified with Christ in His death.

We might have enough of Calvary. We shrink from death and sacrifice. But does Calvary have enough of us? Jesus bids us to follow Him—all the way to Calvary.

a title of liberation

Has a letter ever arrived at your house addressed to your wife as "Ms." instead of "Mrs."? As you know, "Ms." is the new title for women adopted by the Women's Liberation Movement. It means that the woman so addressed does not have to reveal her marital status. Since men don't have to do this, she can in this regard be as independent as any man.

For many years married women have been identified as "Mrs." It seems to have served all right, and most of us might feel that the new title of "Ms." is unnecessary. But it's one by which many women can feel more "liberated."

But speaking of titles for liberation, we all can have one. This title does not designate sex, race, age, or rank. But it's a very liberating title. It shows that one has been set free from sin, self, Satan, and anything else that would limit freedom in any way. That title is "Christian."

Listen to what Paul wrote in Galatians 3:28: "So there is no difference between Jews and Gentiles, between slaves and free men, between men and women: you are all one in union with Christ Jesus" (TEV).

How do you receive this title of liberation? It is by faith in Jesus Christ. Paul also said in Galatians 3:26: "For ye are all children of God by faith in Christ Jesus."

The most liberating title of all is "Christian." It is available to anyone who by faith gives himself to Christ and becomes a child of God.

part two

ABOUT
CHRISTIAN
STEWARDSHIP

hobson's choice
in stewardship

In the seventeenth century, Thomas Hobson rented out horses at Cambridge, England. He had a rule that any person who rented a horse must take the one standing nearest to the stable door.

No matter what station in life the customer held, nor how much he might argue or wheedle, Hobson stuck to his rule.

It did not take long for the expression "Hobson's choice" (which was really no choice at all) to become a familiar statement and pass into colloquial usage.

When it comes to Christian stewardship, "Hobson's choice" is all that we have. We are all stewards. If we are Christians, then we are Christian stewards.

We don't have any decision to make as to *whether* we shall be stewards. Our decision is to decide *what kind* of stewards we will be. We can be good stewards by acknowledging God as the source of all our blessings and returning for His use a portion of our material blessings. Or we can be bad stewards and refuse to part with anything, thinking it all belongs to us. In between the "good" and the "bad" of stewardship are all degrees of stewardship.

A steward basically is one who handles the affairs of another. When we begin with the basic understanding that it is God from whom all blessings flow, then we shall try to serve and honor Him here below.

When it comes to stewardship we have a "Hobson's choice." We already are stewards. From this point we must decide what kind of stewards we are to become.

the most eloquent tithing testimony I ever heard

During the annual stewardship emphasis and budget promotion, many churches have tithing testimonies given by people in the church.

One of the most eloquent testimonies ever shared was not given by a wealthy person. It was not given by a Ph.D. This testimony was given by a state welfare recipient in a little country store.

A little, gray-haired lady in a much washed but freshly ironed cotton dress asked the proprietor to cash her welfare check of fifty-five dollars. In answer to the question of how she wanted the money, she replied, "It doesn't make any difference, just so I have one five-dollar bill and a fifty-cent piece." Then as she wrapped the five-dollar bill around the fifty-cent piece and tucked it into a corner of her purse she explained, "This is my tithe. I always put it by itself so I won't spend it."

Many tithing testimonies have been given. But truly this is one of the most eloquent ever heard.

when heartstrings are touched

When the heartstrings are touched, people respond.

The Lottie Moon Christmas Offering for Foreign Missions often furnishes illustrations of what can happen when the heartstrings are touched. Here are a few examples:

After the 11:00 A.M. service, the pastor was greeting people at one of the doors. A junior high school boy stopped, and handed him a nickel and said, "That's all the money I have. I want it to go to the Lottie Moon

Offering." This is like the widow who gave all the money she had when she gave her mite.

Another boy just had his ninth birthday. An uncle and aunt had given him a check of two dollars. When the money was counted the committee found one Lottie Moon Offering envelope with this personal check for two dollars in it. Across the back, in the finest kind of third grade cursive writing, was the boy's endorsement.

During the week following the offering, a note arrived from a college student with a twenty dollar bill in it. The note indicated that the money was to go to the Lottie Moon Offering. It also said, "Please forgive me for waiting so long. It was practically a necessity that I wait until I received my scholarship money."

When the need is known and the heartstrings are touched, people will do the noble thing. There is no way to estimate the good that can be done for the cause of Christ because of this extra effort of God's people.

There is only one problem: Why are our heartstrings touched so seldom?

Think of all the people we could help; think of all the encouragement we could give; think of all the suffering we could relieve; think of all the witness to Christ we could give; think of all the projects we could complete *if* our heartstrings were touched. Keep your heart in tune with God so that the Holy Spirit can touch your heartstrings.

to whom have you made a sacrifice?

A news article in the New Orleans *Times-Picayune* of April 15, 1969 told of three men in India who had sacrificed a fifty-year-old man to the Hindu goddess in the belief that it would lead them to buried treasure.

This is not the only man in recent years who has been sacrificed for a fortune.

Many men have sacrificed themselves for material gain. Some of them have sacrificed a potentially productive life of service in society for a financially productive but self-centered life. Other men have sacrificed standards and principles for money. For material gain still others have given up a meaningful family life, and thus they have sacrificed their own family for monetary profit.

But is this the sacrifice God intended for us to make?

The New Testament talks about sacrifice, too. In Romans 12:1-2, this statement is found: "So then, my brothers, because of God's many mercies to us, I make this appeal to you: offer yourself as a living sacrifice to God, dedicated to his service and pleasing to him. This is the true worship that you should offer. Do not conform outwardly to the standards of this world, but let God transform you inwardly by a complete change of your mind. Then you will be able to know the will of God——what is good and is pleasing to him, and is perfect" (TEV).

This is the sacrifice we ought to make: not a ritual sacrifice for fortune, but a living sacrifice for service. With this kind of sacrifice we can know God's will and we can serve Christ's cause.

To whom have you made a sacrifice lately? Was it made to something that will not last? Or was it made to God whose will for you is eternal life?

the gospel and giving

A church was in the middle of its emphasis on Christian stewardship when the pastor received a written note from one of the members complaining that all he ever heard about around church was giving, giving, always giving. The pastor wrote in reply, "Thanks for the best definition of Christianity I have ever found: giving, giving, always giving."

16   PEOPLE PARABLES

The gospel and giving are not foreign to each other. They are very closely related.

After all, the gospel had its beginning as a gift—the gift of Jesus Christ, our Savior. The all-time favorite Scripture verse reads, "For God so loved the world, that he gave. . . ."

We receive salvation as a gift from God. Fortunately, God does not give us what we deserve, but rather, what we need. Paul made this clear when he wrote ". . . the gift of God is eternal life through Jesus Christ our Lord."

From beginning to end, Christianity is expressed in giving. The giving of our money is just one part of it. In fact, the money without the man does not amount to much. The gift that God really wants from you is your life. When you give your life to God in complete commital, then you will not object to giving. You will rejoice in giving.

"Giving, giving, always giving." That is a good description of God's grace. As we give of our means to God; as we give our help to others; as we give our witness to the lost; and as we give our lives to the Master, we will see that this rather common complaint is really a good description of Christianity: "Giving, giving, always giving."

something to remember when you give to the church

Harry Emerson Fosdick once told of a major women's college that was conducting a financial campaign. A wealthy and prominent alumna was asked by the committee to send a message to back up their appeal. "Make it happy," instructed the committee, "something to cheer us up." The alumna wrote back that she was glad to send a message, but that she could not make it happy. "Tell them this for me," she wrote. "Never take your college for granted! A lot of people broke their hearts to give it to you." To this Fosdick added, "That's true about the church."

That's true about the church universal. It's also true about each local congregation.

This one thought gives much meaning to a good theme for stewardship emphasis: "Give . . . in the spirit of Christ."

Christ gave His life for us. Surely, in loving response to that great gift of grace, we will give worthy gifts.

The worthy gift starts with the person. We must first give ourselves to Christ. Then what monetary gift we present will become an effective expression of our gratitude to God.

When we consider that a lot of people broke their hearts to give us the church, and that Christ gave His life to give us our salvation, we cannot be flippant or unconcerned or smug about our Christian stewardship—we dare not!

be careful
whom you rob

An elderly Baptist deacon, after speaking at evening service, was handed two one-dollar bills. These he placed carefully in his billfold and started back to his home afoot. At the edge of the town, he was suddenly confronted by a man with a big handkerchief over his face and a pistol in his hand.

"Give me your money," snarled the robber, "before I blow you in two with this gun."

Terrified, the deacon shot both hands into the air as high as he could, and he said, "Please, Mr. Robber, just reach into my back pocket and get my billfold out, but don't shoot me!"

The robber reached one hand around the trembling deacon and jerked out the billfold. Turning his light upon it, he opened it. He found the two one-dollar bills and a card. The card had the deacon's name on it plus these words, "A Baptist Layman for Christ."

"Are you a member of a Baptist church?" questioned the robber.

"Yes, sir, I am a Baptist deacon and I do supply preaching."

"Well, here," said the robber. "Take this money back, I'm a Baptist myself."

All Baptists aren't that careful about whom they rob.

Baptists who do not give regularly through their church rob other Baptists of the ministry that the church can perform. As they shift more of the burden of financial support upon other church members they also rob them.

But they rob Baptists around the world, too. Baptist work in all the world suffers when an individual Baptist is not faithful financially. And they rob themselves of the joys and privileges in participating through their money in exciting things for Christ.

But a prophet long ago really expressed it when he said, "Will a man rob God? Yet ye have robbed me. But ye say, Wherein have we robbed thee? In tithes and offerings" (Mal. 3:8).

When you start to make out your pledge card be careful that you don't rob.

how God loses nickels

A little boy was given two nickels by his mother one Sunday morning and was told that one was to go into the Sunday school offering and the other could be spent as he pleased. Walking down the street and feeling very affluent, he was tossing one of the coins into the air when he dropped it. The coin rolled off the gutter into a drain and was lost. The boy looked very sad for a moment, and then he brightened up and said, "Sorry, Lord, I lost Your nickel."

God loses a lot of nickels that way.

Many people give God only what is left over after they have spent money as they pleased. They expect the Lord to suffer the main losses.

If the tithe is the Lord's as the Bible says, then the Lord's nickels have been spent on a lot that is not the Lord's business. The Lord loses a lot of nickels that way.

Many of the Lord's nickels are spent at the State Fair, at places of amusement, or at restaurants.

Some of the Lord's nickels are spent on vacations, weekend trips, or hunting expeditions.

There have been times when the Lord's money has gone for food, clothing, automobiles, or appliances.

Whenever a part of your money is lost or wasted or spent, and you have to say, "Well, Lord, there's no money left over for You," it explains how God loses nickels.

if you really care . . . share

When Alaska experienced a terrible earthquake a few years ago, the governor's wife reported that many letters of request came to the governor's mansion. She answered most of them, and usually they were demands that she do something for some relative or some friend. But she received one letter from the Midwest, from a ten-year-old boy who enclosed two nickels. "If you need any more," he wrote, "please let me know."

This young man was ready to share because he cared.

And this very attitude gets right to the heart of Christian stewardship. It is because of a caring love, that we are willing to share what we have.

We really care about the spread of the gospel . . . so we share.

We really care about human need . . . so we share.

We really care about our young people . . . so we share.

We really care about ministry in our community . . . so we share.

We really care about our church . . . so we share.

God cares for us. He cares so much that Jesus died on the cross for us. He providentially cares for us day after day. Our response to His love should be our love. We express our Christian love by our caring . . . for Him and for others.

If you really care, then share. That's a pretty good theme for a stewardship emphasis. It gets down to bedrock. So look at your own heart. See how much you care. Then share.

to pledge
or not to pledge

As a part of a stewardship campaign someone once wrote this amusing parody on the words of Shakespeare:

To pledge or not to pledge—that is the question.
Whether 'tis nobler in a man
To take the gospel free and let another foot the bill,
Or sign a pledge and pay toward church expenses!
To give, to pay—aye, there's the rub. To pay,
When on the free-pew plan, a man may have
A sitting free and take the gospel, too,
As though he paid, and none be aught the wiser
Save the Finance Committee, who—
Most honorable of men—can keep a secret!
To err is human, and human, too, to buy
At cheapest rate. I'll take the gospel so!
For others do the same—a common rule!
I'm wise. I'll wait, not work—I'll pray, not pay,
And let the other fellow foot the bills,
And so I'll get the gospel free, you see!

Most Baptist churches have a Dedication Day. On this day church members are asked that they return their pledge cards and indicate on them the measure of their financial support for the church's ministry during the next year.

The basic purpose is not simply to underwrite the budget. Rather, the basic purpose is to help individual Christians to become involved in sharing in the blessings of the gospel and in sharing their material blessings for the work of the gospel.

"To pledge or not to pledge"—this is your question. I trust that you will pledge. It will help you to nail down your commitment. It will help the church to have some idea of where it is going next year.

"To pledge or not to pledge"—please do. You won't regret it.

my father's stewardship testimony

My father died in 1965. For many years he had been a Baptist deacon, as was his father before him.

My father took his Christian faith very seriously. To him stewardship was an important part of Christianity. And, to him, stewardship meant tithing. No matter what else had to wait, he made sure that the Lord received His tithe.

I don't know that I ever heard him put it in these words, but I think my father would have said that he practiced tithing for three reasons: the Bible taught it, it was God's will, and it was right. This combination of reasons was convincing enough for him.

Tithing did not insure for my father a long life. He died at sixty-two years of age, which isn't a ripe old age these days.

Tithing did not make my father wealthy. At his death he did not leave much wealth, a lot of insurance, or vast land holdings. Although we always had food, clothing, and shelter, our family was far from being wealthy. Dad worked long, hard hours all his life.

And tithing did not keep bad things from happening to him. We had our share of the crises that typically fall upon all families. My father died from cancer after eighteen months of suffering and several rounds of surgery.

If tithing did not make my father wealthy or insure him of a long life or keep him from suffering, why did he tithe? He did it because he thought it was what he should do as a Christian. Since the Bible taught it, he felt that it was God's will and that it was right. Dad faithfully tithed without wavering.

By the way, part of the legacy my father left me was the memory and influence of a strong, vital, practicing Christian faith—as well as a tithing testimony.

holding the ropes

The first society for the work of foreign missions was formed in 1792 in England. The society was born out of the missionary impulse of William Carey and his eloquent, insistent pleas that Baptists should do something for the conversion of the heathen. When the missionary society was formed because of Carey's efforts, he offered himself as the first missionary.

In 1791, he had published a little book entitled *An Inquiry into the Obligations of Christians to Use Means for the Conversion of the Heathen*. In 1792, he preached this famous message, based on Isaiah 54:2-3, at the Nottinghamshire Baptist Association. In October of 1792, at the home of a Widow Wallis, the mission society was formed and the modern mission movement began. In offering himself as a missionary, Carey said to the men, "I will go down into the well, if you will hold the ropes." By holding the ropes he meant for them to give him financial and prayer support.

This is what we are doing through Christian stewardship. We are holding the ropes for all that Christ is doing through the churches.

We cannot all go as missionaries, either to Tanzania, the ghettos of New York City, or to Mamou; but we can hold the ropes for those who do go.

We cannot all preach or direct the youth programs in a church, but we can hold the ropes for those who do.

We cannot all work directly with the children in a Baptist Children's Home, but we can hold the ropes for those who do.

We cannot all guide the children in our church's teaching and music ministry, but we can hold the ropes for those who do.

It is important for somebody to go down into the well. And it is essential that someone hold the ropes. This we can all do through the practice of Christian stewardship.

part three

ABOUT
CHRISTIAN
MINISTRY

a chance you have to take

One spring day as flood waters rose in a nearby river, a farmer was frantically working with the bees that he had in hives at the back of his yard. The water had already gotten into some of the hives and drowned some bees. A neighbor saw him, climbed the fence, and helped him move the rest of the bees to higher ground. As the helpful neighbor straightened up after the last box had been moved, a bee stung him right on the back of the neck.

Now someone might say, "See, that's what I thought all the time. You try to help someone and you get stung. It happens every time!" It is true that sometimes when you try to help someone you will get stung. But that's a chance you've got to take.

Whenever you start talking about helping other people or ministering to them in the name of Christ, someone is sure to remind you of all the times he has gotten stung. He gave someone some money—and it was spent on liquor. He helped someone get a job—and he quit after two days. He fed some hungry family—and they gave the food away because they didn't like the brand of beans. He gave some clothing to an inadequately clothed family—and they threw them away rather than wash them. But even when you get stung in serving in Christ's name, it is a chance you have to take.

The Lord never assured us that what we do for others would be adequately used or even appreciated. But He did tell us that to minister we must. Anytime you try to help another you run the risk of getting stung. But it is a chance you have to take. When it is successful and helps another it is all worth it. Why don't you take the chance?

think small

On the front of the tiny match folder, distributed by a Volkswagen dealer, is a picture of the "bug" and the words "think small."

Sometimes we do need to think small. This seems strange to say in our day of grandiose schemes and super planning. But often the very enormity of what we see around us baffles us and freezes us into inaction.

For, you see, we can be so overwhelmed by what we see and hear that we walk right by our immediate opportunities. And often it is because we are thinking "big" instead of thinking "small."

We look at the overwhelming problems of our world —poverty, hunger, racism, pollution, war, revolution —and think, "What can one person do?" We look at big problems and think that there must be big answers. To cure these ills on a world-wide scale would take big solutions.

But not one of us is called upon to cure these ills on a worldwide scale. We can work on them right where we are. We can fight poverty, hunger, racism, pollution, and hate right where we are. But we have to think small to do it.

We can begin with some of our own attitudes. We can show interest and concern. We can find some individuals who need our help and ministry, and begin to work in a very limited way with them. The big problem overwhelms us while the small solution is so close to us we often miss it.

What can I do to help the problems of people? I can begin by thinking small.

"I helping Jesus . . ."

While I was sweeping fallen leaves off the porch, Chyrisse, my four-year-old daughter, attempted to help by raking the porch floor. I suggested she not do that because the paint would be scratched. She left the porch, but while she walked along the sidewalk dragging the rake behind her, she said to me, "I helping Jesus."

She had learned that when a little girl helps her daddy she helps Jesus. And this is precisely what Jesus Himself said. He told a story illustrating the Judgment. Those who were assigned to the places of blessing were those whose character was such that, without being self-conscious about it or even conscious of it, they had helped other people. By helping other people they had helped Jesus.

This principle is our mandate to minister. All around us are people who need our ministry. They are older people who feel lonely and forgotten. They are the sick people who have pain and discomfort. They are the young people struggling with momentous decisions. They are the students facing daily crises as their eyes are opened and their horizons are expanded. They are the poor, the neglected, the disturbed, and the forgotten.

We can help them in hundreds of meaningful ways. It does not take all that much effort. But it does take some time, some caring, some interest, and some direction.

How good it would be if, while walking through life, we could say with assurance, "I helping Jesus."

people is what it's all about

Every once in a while we get the idea that some folks think that everything would go along just fine if it were not for people. People interrupt them. People bother them. People bring problems to them. People take up their time.

But people is what it's all about. The teacher who complains about the people forgets that his job is to teach people. The physician who is upset about people forgets that his commission is to heal people. The merchant who gripes about people forgets that he is there to serve people. The minister who is bothered by the people forgets that his calling is to be a pastor to people.

Especially when we think of the church we are reminded that people is what it is all about. The church, and everyone who seeks to serve God by serving in the church, is to try to meet the needs of people. We are to teach people, to witness to people, to lead people into deeper spiritual experiences, and to minister to the needs of people. It all focuses on how we bring the revelation and redemption of God to bear on people and their needs.

This means that each individual is extremely important. We are to think of persons and not of just people in general. One of the great truths of God's love that Jesus expressed is that God is interested in each person. And so must we be interested in each person.

Some people are wearing little lapel buttons that include these words: "Please do not mutilate, fold, or spindle. I am a person."

We ought to remember that message. People is what it's all about.

people lovers are hard to find

Some years ago there was a Jack Clayton Appreciation Banquet at the Northwestern State University of Louisiana student center. Many gathered to honor Coach Jack Clayton who had just left Northwestern State University after eleven years as athletic director, nine years of which he was also head football coach.

Among the speakers was Charlie Hennigan, who went from NSU to fame as a professional football player. In his closing remarks Dr. Hennigan said, "He's a people lover. And people lovers are hard to find."

People lovers are hard to find. It costs to be a people lover. You may have to get involved in the lives of others. You cannot be a strict isolationist. Neither can you just categorize people. You will have to take them as individuals, judge them as individuals, and deal with them as individuals. You will have to genuinely care for people.

But people lovers are desperately needed. Christian service, both individual and institutional, would completely bog down without people lovers. Ministry to others in its various forms demands people lovers. Loving people is the basis for Christian witness.

Unfortunately, people lovers are hard to find. Too often we would prefer to go our way, hoe our own row, do our own thing without bothering with people.

I wish this great compliment could be truthfully said about each one of us: "He's a people lover." This is exactly what Jesus is. This is what we must be.

a lesson about leadership

A veterinarian and his helpers were trying to get some cattle into a chute to give them some medication. They tried and tried to drive them through the gate that led to the chute. But it was all to no avail—they could not get them in. So they stood off to the side to rest awhile before starting to drive them again. While they were resting with their arms folded, the cattle voluntarily went through the gate one by one. Then they tried that for their method. They would drive the cattle only to the gate, then stand aside, and the cattle would voluntarily enter the gate.

This tells us a lot about leadership. You can lead people much better than you can drive them.

We often try to drive people to do the things we want. Driving may take the form of coercion, pressures, or threats. The goal you have in mind in what you are trying to get them to do may be good. It may be the best thing for them to do. But the method used often defeats the goal.

Why not try leading instead of driving? Show the need. Lay the burden on the person or persons involved. Convince them of the beneficial results of that particular action. Then lead them to the decision.

Cattle are not always easily driven. Neither are people. In all of our leadership efforts, at whatever level of leadership we operate, we can get better and more lasting results by leading rather than driving.

our commitment
and our job

A cartoon in the *New Yorker* magazine pictured two rather seedy looking students walking across a college campus. One of them, disheveled, with beard, and hair awry, looked at the other one and said, "I have a desperate need for commitment, and what happens?" Then he answered his own question, "I'm offered a job."

As Christians, our commitment determines our job. When Jesus Christ is accepted as Lord and Savior of life, the grandest kind of commitment takes place. Out of this commitment grows the job we have.

Our commitment determines our job of personal development. Each of us has a goal in life—to grow to be more like Jesus Christ, our Lord. Christian growth, however, is not automatic. It is our job daily to try to make the characteristics of the life of Christ the characteristics of our lives.

Our commitment determines our job as personal witnesses. The very nature of the salvation experience demands that this experience be shared. In our jobs, in our homes, in our social contacts, we share the experience by sharing the new kind of life we find in Christ. Witnessing does not have to be structured. But it does have to be Christian.

Rather than becoming disgusted when we need commitment and find a job, we can clearly see that our Christian commitment determines our job. Let us do this job with all the strength God gives us.

from the abstract
to the concrete

A drunk fell in a sidewalk of wet cement and then just stayed there for the rest of the night sleeping it off. The next morning the cement had hardened around him. After they had finally chipped him out, he said, "Getting drunk is fine in the abstract, but it's not so good in the concrete."

Many of our ideas and ideals are much the same. They are fine in the abstract, when we just sit around and talk about them. But to get them into the concrete, into action out in the world, often is something else entirely. This is a constant problem with religious ideas and impulses.

Take, for instance, the concept of ministry. A denomination decides that for a year it will place strong emphasis on ministry. They want to involve all of their people actively in ministry. That's fine in the abstract, but how do you get it into the concrete?

You get it into the concrete by actively seeking ways that the individual can serve others to help meet their needs both through single actions and in sustaining activities. You do it by gathering food, clothing, cooking utensils to send to neighbors in another state who have had their belongings ruined and their lives upset through the tragedy of a hurricane or flood. You do it through an extension Sunday school class in a geriatrics hospital.

These actions don't have to be spectacular. A lot of old people need someone who will just "sit and visit a spell." Someone may need transportation to and from a doctor's office. A sick mother may need her child cared for.

Ministry is a magnificent idea in the abstract. It is even better in the concrete. Keep your eyes open. There are hundreds of ways you can change your service from the abstract to the concrete.

what can one person do?

A question that often comes to mind when talking about Christian witness and Christian service is, "Well, what can one person do?"

Often because the voice of one person does not seem very strong, nothing is done. There is a little poem that speaks to this problem.

> I am only one,
> But still I am one.
> I cannot do everything,
> But still I can do something.
> I will not refuse to do something
> That I can do.

Each person can do only the things that one person can do. But if each one of us does those things, it can make an impact.

What can you do? You can be sure that you have a functioning faith in Christ. You can perform acts of thoughtfulness and kindness when people are sick, are troubled, or are distressed. You can speak positive words of Christian witness: quote Bible verses, mark a New

Testament, or give your own personal testimony. You can show genuine concern.

You can do innumerable things. But you must do them! Too long have we talked about ministering in Christ's name but have not done it. Now is the time to act.

What can one person do? One person can do a lot. Imagination and concern will open many doors.

because we care

Little tags that were put on the outside of each box and put inside the clothing read, "Because We Care. . . ." Then followed a verse of Scripture, either Mark 10:41, Matthew 10:42, John 3:16, Proverbs 3:5-6, Romans 5:1, or John 14:27. After this came the name and address of the church.

The following morning it was all loaded on a truck and sent to Corpus Christi, Texas, for relief of the victims of Hurricane Celia.

"Because we care. . . ." This must always be the motivation for ministry performed in the name of Jesus Christ.

For ministry to be effective it must not be ". . . because we must," or ". . . because we can," or ". . . because we will," but ". . . because we care."

Because we care, we will help whenever we can. Then we will feel compassion. Then we will have the will to serve. But caring must come first. Caring is the foundation upon which Christian personal ministry is built.

When C. W. Brister was preparing to write his book entitled *People Who Care*, he mentioned the title to a friend who replied dubiously, "You mean there are still some of those people around?" As long as there are Christians around, there will be some of those people around. People who care stand at the very heart of Christian ministry.

"Because we care. . . ." That is why we witness, serve, share, and minister. It must always be our motivation.

we believe in people!
spread that word

A striking radio advertisement for a finance company said, "When you believe in people the word gets around." Its message is a good one. It would do fine for any church.

Because a church is in business for God, it must deal with people. Since it deals with people the church also must believe in people. What you believe about God will show up in how you treat people.

A church must believe that people are significant, that each person has worth and dignity. Having been made in the image of God, each person has particular value. Of all people, church people cannot afford a low view of man.

Each person becomes important to them. It is by a personal experience that each individual is related to God. We cannot be so taken up with the masses that we miss the individuals. We cannot count by tens or hundreds or thousands and fail to count by ones. Each person counts.

An English reformer, who had led in the passage of many laws that benefitted the common person, received a letter asking him to help in a certain case. He replied that he had been so busy helping the people that he could not be concerned about a person. What a contradiction!

A church, then, must focus its attention on people. People are important. People are more important than our programs, because the program must exist for people rather than people existing for the program.

Let us be sure that the word gets around: "We believe in people!"

We are attempting to reach people for Christ, to develop people as Christians, to train people as Christian ministers, to inspire people to be Christian witnesses, and to bring the Word of God to bear on people's lives. We believe in people! We believe that God is interested in people! We must always be people-centered in our approach to the Christian ministry.

Spread that word.

our ministry

You would find something very significant in the Sunday bulletin of the City Church of the Brethren, Goshen, Indiana. Above the order of service are these words:

City Church of the Brethren
Goshen, Indiana
Ministers—The People of City Church
Pastor—Nevin H. Zuck

Now this is 100 percent Biblical. It is a true expression of the ministry of the Christian. Actually, all of us are ministers; even though one of us has been chosen for the particular function of the ministry as a pastor.

When I read that, I thought of something the apostle Paul wrote to the Christians in Ephesus. He said, "It is he who 'gave gifts to men'; he appointed some to be apostles, others to be prophets, others to be evangelists, others to be pastors and teachers. He did this to prepare all God's people for the work of Christian service, to build up the body of Christ" (Eph. 4:11-12 TEV).

Our ministry is given to us by God. Some of us can do some things better than others. We have a diversity of gifts but a single purpose: to build up the body of Christ.

The problem that we face as Christians is that we have difficulty in our ministry. More of us acknowledge it than accept it.

If we accept the ministry that God has given us, then we will seek to minister in Christ's name and by His power through the gifts that He has given us to meet human need. It is a task for all of us.

Who are the ministers of your church? Why, you and all the rest of the members are. Let us accept the ministry God has given to us.

part four

ABOUT
CHRISTIAN
LIFE

the dreadful duty
of the defense

On the way home from the basketball tournament in which his team had won its first game, Craig was excitedly discussing the game with his father. He was telling about the plays and the patterns they were trying to run. Then he said, "But they were always messing up our plays." With all the basketball wisdom of his accumulated years his father replied, "Well, son, that's the job of the defense. They are supposed to try to mess up your plays."

Isn't it awful? In all of life someone is always around to mess up our plays. The greatest financial problems come from the unexpected expenditures. Some big disappointments come from plans that we were not able to carry out. Keen discouragements come from the discoveries that all of life is not going to develop just as we had mapped it out. Demoralizing personal defeats come when people stand in our way. Somebody is always messing up our plays.

To be a Christian does not mean that no one will ever mess up your plays. The defense begins to try even harder then. The forces of evil exert their efforts even more strongly against the Christian.

But being a Christian does mean that even when the plays are messed up the game goes on. We will still try to stand for right and the will of God. The dreadful duty of the defense is to try to mess up our plays. The glorious opportunity of the offense is to continue in moving forward for Christ.

a balanced diet
and spiritual growth

Keith is in the second grade. His class at school has taken up a unit on health. He came rushing home that first day to inform all the members of his household what he was supposed to eat each day. At supper he enumerated everything he had eaten that day, and then asked for an orange, a slice of bread, and another glass of milk. The next morning, he not only ate his bowl of cereal but he also ordered an egg. His mother always has been extremely careful that her family has balanced meals. And Keith takes vitamins on top of that. There was no danger that Keith's diet was deficient. But he was going to make certain he had all he needed.

What would happen if people were that concerned about their spiritual health?

Some principles of spiritual health are well known to all of us. Each day we need some Bible reading, some prayer, some reflection, some sharing of faith. Added to that we must have the corporate worship services, the exercise of stewardship, some meaningful service, and the development of the Christian graces. However, we usually do not work quite so hard to see that we have all of these elements in our lives.

Physical well-being? Yes, we will make sure our diets are balanced and adequate. Spiritual well-being? That we all too often leave to chance. Wouldn't it be nice if we tried for a wholesome balanced diet for all of life—both physical and spiritual?

too much of a good thing

A family went on vacation to the Ozark Mountains. The two boys in the family decided they would like to go fishing for rainbow trout. Of the available alternatives, the least expensive way to fish seemed to be to fish in the trout pond and pay only for the fish caught.

For a time it seemed that this would be an extremely inexpensive way to fish because they had not caught a thing. Then they learned the technique, and the two went to work catching fish. Before Dad realized what was happening and could call a quick halt to it, the two boys had caught $11.85 worth of rainbow trout. Rainbow trout are fun to catch and good to eat, but that was too much of a good thing.

We all have the problem of balance from time to time. We misuse many things that are good until we discover that perhaps we have had too much of a good thing.

Sometimes it happens with recreational activities. A person realizes one day (or, as a part of the problem, he does not realize it) that he is spending most of his time, energy, and effort at one activity. More worthy things suffer because of it.

Those folk who are called religious fanatics (I really do not know how to define a religious fanatic and apparently no one else does either) are people who, supposedly, have too much of a good thing.

A balance in life is what we need: enough work, enough rest, enough recreation, enough outside activity. But be sure you achieve a balance. You really do not have a balanced life without a wholesome and adequate spiritual emphasis.

it comes with no warning

The young hunter was all excited. He had gone hunting in the Red Dirt Game Management Area of the Kisatchie National Forest. The spot he picked for his stand was on a slope looking down over a clear area. Between two trees on a little dump of dirt he sat. About 8:30 in the morning three hunters had already walked by him. When the last pair passed he said to himself, "Shucks, there is too much traffic. I won't do any good here." And he got up to move. While he was stepping down from his little dirt dump, off balance, with his gun in his left hand, thoroughly unprepared, suddenly a deer materialized about thirty or forty yards ahead of him. There he stood face to face with the deer. They must have seen one another about the same time. The young hunter hurriedly threw up his gun and shot and missed.

One thing is sure about deer. They do not give any advance warning that they are coming.

The same thing is true about temptation to sin. It comes with no warning. It would help tremendously if we had some kind of moral Distant Early Warning system to alert us that temptation was on its way. But we do not. Temptation comes before we know it and often it comes from unexpected places.

Since we do not have any advance warning about temptation we must always be alert. We can never be half-asleep at our stand. We cannot afford to be off-balance.

Paul once said, "So take up God's armor now! Then when the evil day comes, you will be able to resist the enemy's attacks, and often fighting to the end, you will still hold your ground" (Eph. 6:13 TEV). That is still very good advice, because temptation many times comes with no warning.

when you are out of step

What is your reaction to Daylight Saving Time? Betty did not like it, so she just simply refused to abide by it. She would not change her clock. For the most part, she was out of step with the whole nation. And she didn't care.

Sometimes we find ourselves in situations in which it seems that we are out of step with everybody else.

When that happens we need to examine why we are

out of step. There are times when it might be simply because we are stubborn, or cranky, or cantankerous. There are times when it might be because of a strong conviction to which we have prayerfully come and which we fondly hold. And sometimes it can be that a person is marching to the beat of a distant drummer. But when we find ourselves out of step with everyone else we need to examine ourselves. The cause could be with us instead of with them.

Then we will want to make whatever adjustments are necessary. If the cause is our own fault, we may need to make some changes in our attitudes, our actions, or our outlook. If we feel that we cannot make the change ourselves then we can find ways to deal kindly with those who differ with us, to love other people, and to express our reasons tactfully.

Christians often will find themselves out of step with some things going on around them. But keep your conviction and be able to witness through it.

This fine lady will probably go to bed and get up at the same time she always has. But as far as the clock is concerned, she will be out of step with the rest of the nation. Sometimes this is good. But sometimes we need to think about getting in step—for that may be the way God is moving.

"round and round she goes, where she stops . . ."

A man decided to ride a merry-go-round at a carnival. When the ride was over his wife sized him up with her hands on her hips and then said, "Now look at you. You done spent your nickel. You got off where you got on. And you ain't been nowhere yet!"

This could be the summary statement of life for many people. Round and round life goes. But when it all stops, where have they been?

Oh, time has been filled, all right. The hours have been packed with all kind of activities. There have been meetings, clubs, organizations, and societies galore. But where has it taken them? Have they moved a world, or a family, or even one life toward higher standards and greater achievement? Have they realized some goals? Have they deepened their spiritual life, broadened their understanding of God, heightened their appreciation of Biblical truths, or lengthened their perception of spiritual truths?

Things continue to go round and round. Sometimes life goes around at such a speed that we can hardly keep up. One of our biggest tasks as Christians is to see that there is continual advancement toward our goal of Christlikeness. We cannot afford to get off where we got on without going anywhere.

how do you look at things?

It's a fact that people tend to put their own problems first. This is vividly illustrated by a story which Paul C. Smith tells.

Smith was heading up *Collier's* magazine in the days just before it folded, and he decided to call a full staff meeting to explain why the "ship" was sinking. He even invited the stenographers and the mailroom girls.

At the meeting, Smith held nothing back. He told of *Collier's* six-million-dollar debt, of its falling sales, and of the two million dollars that somehow had to be raised. He talked for three hours.

"And that's the fix we're in," he concluded. "Now are there any questions?"

"Yes," said a secretary from the back of the room. "Why can't the Schrafft's coffee wagon come to the thirteenth floor?"

Christian faith demands that we take our eyes off ourselves and our concerns and look at the needs of others. We are to be concerned about them, interested in them, and active for them. The very example of the Savior who gave His life for us demands that we must be concerned with more than just ourselves and our problems. How do you look at things?

our relation to one another

Recently, the papers carried the news of a tragedy in Argentina. A dam broke and the rushing waters drowned several people. For the most part those who read the news, thought, "My, that's bad," and put the paper aside, thinking that it did not concern them.

But it did concern all of us. Philosophically it concerned us because we are related to all people in the world. Their misery is our misery.

So often we fail to get concerned about a tragedy unless we are directly involved in it. If it is somewhere else we just dismiss it. But true concern doesn't limit itself geographically. Even if it is not one of our neighbors, nonetheless someone has suffered loss, someone is hurting. And it should concern us.

We are all related to one another. John Donne expressed it three centuries or so ago: "No man is an island, entire of itself; every man is a piece of the continent, a part of the main; if a clod be washed away by the sea, Europe is the less, as well as if a promontory were, as well as if a manor of thy friends or of thine own were. Any man's death diminishes me, because I am involved in mankind. And therefore never send to know for whom the bell tolls; it tolls for thee."

Every once in awhile we need to be reminded again of this truth.

hiding in the hydrangeas

Late one Saturday afternoon, Dad walked out the back door with a water pail in one hand. In the other was soap, a brush, and dip. It was bath time for Punkin, the family dog. That was Dad's job.

Usually Punkin runs to meet anyone coming out the door. This time he started toward the door, spied what Dad had in his hands, then took off around the corner of the house. When Dad got to the bottom step and called him, Punkin poked his head around the corner. Then they didn't see him again.

The children tried to help Dad find him. Finally they found him lying very flat and very still in a hole he had hollowed out under a hydrangea bush. Hiding in the hydrangeas, Punkin was trying to escape the inevitable.

How often we have hid in our own particular variety of hydrangea in an attempt to do just that—escape the inevitable.

Sometimes there are problems we have to face. We know they are there, but we hedge in every way we can. We just don't want to face up to them.

Death is an inevitability of life. We all are born sometime to die. But we rarely apply this personally. It is always someone else who will die. So we put off making decisions, righting the wrongs, and changing our lives.

There is much in our lives that should be changed. God often tries to break through, but we won't let Him. Forgiveness is needed, but repentance comes first. And so often we will not do it. We will not face the inevitable about our own lives.

Hiding in the hydrangeas will not keep us from facing the inevitable. Face it we must. Let's prepare for it while we can.

part five
ABOUT
THE
CHRISTIAN
CHURCH

an incredible claim

On the edge of a small Arkansas town stands a church building. The building needs painting. The roof is sagging. The yard is unkempt. The windows are dirty. But just in front of the building is a sign that proclaims the following message in large, nonprofessionally painted letters: "WELCOME TO THE POWERHOUSE." The name of the church follows.

Those who read the sign and see the building are sure to think, "What an incredible claim! How could anyone claim this as a powerhouse?"

But isn't the whole claim of the Christian faith incredible? We are claiming exactly what that sign proclaims. Any church can be a powerhouse for God. Any Christian can be the instrument of God's power.

The whole secret of Christianity is that God's Holy Spirit can work in ordinary people, and from this comes extraordinary results. The Christian must be a person whose life's power comes from God and not from himself.

Yes, it is an incredible claim. But it is the claim that any Christian and any church can make. When the Holy Spirit is present, any church can be a powerhouse.

a loss of power and the renewing of power

The summer school students at Northwestern State University got an unexpected vacation one week when classes were canceled due to a power failure on the campus. It seems that the transformer of a major electrical substation blew out. This left eight buildings on the west side of the campus without electricity. That part of the campus lost its power.

But this is not the first time an institution has lost its power.

History is cluttered with the fragile shells of once powerful institutions. These institutions began with a mighty show of power, only to lose their power somewhere along the way.

Power is lost when the reason for being—the basic purpose—is not fully understood or is obstructed by side issues. Old age, refusal to change, or inability to adapt to new situations have all contributed to the loss of power.

Today, some people think that the church as an institution has lost its power. They can point to many indications and say, "The power is gone. The church is dying."

You need not join this bunch of gloomy announcers of doom. We have always said, "Where there is life there is hope." The church of our Lord Jesus Christ is far from dead. There is life. And that means there is hope.

Northwestern State University got new power when a new transformer was installed. Both the church and individual Christians will get new power when there is full dependence on the Source of power. For the Christian church, the source of power is God. When there is full dependence on God's Holy Spirit, there is a renewing of power.

In many ways, the best days for the church may be ahead. This can be true with a renewing of power by dependence on God.

a matter of perspective

One of the recent nonfiction best sellers is a book entitled, *A Modern Priest Looks at His Outdated Church*, by Father James Kavanaugh. Now don't immediately think, "Hey, this is an inside exposé of the Catholic Church." It is not intended to be that at all. And it shouldn't be read as that.

While it is true that Father Kavanaugh is an angry young man with some noticeable "hang ups," he also says some things that all of us who are associated with churches ought to notice. He is very concerned with the individual and the freedom of the individual.

He did not outline them in this way, but there are three problems that he approaches that deal with the individual. These are things about which we should also want to be careful.

Putting law above love is one problem area. We can be so strict in the carrying out of certain "laws" that we forget the love that the Bible indicates as the supreme law. Laws are important, but love is essential. We may not have "church laws" as such, but we can sometimes get some very strong traditions.

Emphasizing policies (or programs) above persons is another problem area. Jesus showed us that the person is extremely important. We must always be concerned with the needs, the struggles, and the problems of the person.

In addition, putting institutions above individuals is an ever-present danger. Our institutions help us to carry on our programs. But the programs and the institutions are intended to serve the individual, not vice versa. You will remember that Jesus Himself ran into some difficulty with others over that point.

It is a matter of perspective. In it all, we surely want to keep our perspective, to love the individual, and to seek to serve persons through Jesus Christ.

deadly diseases for churches

In his book, *The Reputation of a Church*, G. Avery Lee, pastor of the Saint Charles Avenue Baptist Church, New

Orleans, lists four diseases that kill a church. He said that these four diseases are: "sleeping sickness," "cirrhosis of the giver," "hardening of the heartaries," and "spiritual myopia."

Let's examine each one of these.

For a church to be afflicted by "sleeping sickness" is to be asleep amid possibilities. Isn't that tragic for a church? Consider some of the possibilities that we have for outreach to university students, townspeople, young married couples, and young people. Consider some of the possibilities we have for ministry to aged persons, to disadvantaged people, and to the neglected. Consider the talent and the resources we have available to us. We surely have the possibilities for Christian service and growth. We must not be asleep to them.

The church with "cirrhosis of the giver" suffers from an improper stewardship. This church may depend only on certain persons to give. Or it may depend largely on outside sources for its money. But the strongest stewardship churches are those in which all the members feel a responsibility and support the church through regular giving.

Another deadly disease for a church is "hardening of the heartaries." This is due to a lack of concern. Compassionate concern for persons marked the life and ministry of Jesus. The church, the body of Christ, must have this same degree of concern. It is inconceivable that a church could be unconcerned about people's problems, their relationship to God, and their spiritual development. Too often, churches have been concerned only about themselves and their welfare without exhibiting a real concern for others.

A church with "spiritual myopia" sees only the immediate. It is unwilling to take the long look and to consider its responsibility in the days ahead. Short-sighted decisions, failure to provide space and property for expansion, and refusal to have meaningful children's programs or youth ministries can ultimately be fatal for such a church. To save a few dollars, a church can sometimes sell out its future.

Make your own diagnosis. Do you want to keep your church healthy and free of any of these diseases? Preventive medicine is the best approach. How about helping to practice it?

worshiping in an unfinished church

A congregation was worshiping in an unfinished church building while the auditorium was being renovated. It was disconcerting at times for the people to look around and see the exposed lumber, unpainted walls, and uncovered platform surfaces. The new baptistry was just sitting up there with only framing around it. And when they looked up there were naked light bulbs hanging down from where the light fixtures were to be. It was all a little disconcerting because this is not what is normally expected in a church building. We expect churches to be finished and clean and straight.

But spiritually speaking, the church is never finished!

The church is always in the process of becoming. We never have absolutely ascertained the will of God. We never have completely understood the work of the Holy Spirit. We never have fully realized what God is trying to tell us. We never have certainly known the direction God is trying to move us.

Some churches have been finished. They have frozen doctrine into creeds. They have locked worship into ritual and liturgy. They have hemmed in the Holy Spirit to certain forms. Because of it, both the churches and the people have suffered.

Paul Tillich identified the Reformation principle as the ability of the church to keep on reforming itself. This is absolutely essential if the church is to be the living, vital, growing organism that God intended.

A "live-in" renovation is sometimes inconvenient. But a "finished" church would be even worse. Let us seek to always be open to the leadership of God's Spirit so that we can truly be the people of God at this time and in this place.

sin in the church

Several years ago the District 8 Baptist Convention was holding its annual convention at the First Baptist Church in the town of Converse, Louisiana. Miss Myra Gulledge, BSU director at Northwestern State, was in attendance at the meeting. She had brought along her well-loved and well-known pet dog, "Sin." Since most churches don't allow dogs in the building, Myra had left Sin out in the car.

During Myra's report of the activities of the BSU during the foregoing year she suddenly stopped and said frantically, "There's Sin in the church!" Someone jumped up and said, "What?" Another chimed in, "Who?" And all the while Sin was unconcernedly trotting down the middle aisle.

Well, "Sin" was promptly apprehended and properly dispatched, and the meeting went on as usual. Frankly, though, the shocked reaction at sin in the church should set us to thinking.

The first question asked was a good one. What sin is there in the church? We must examine ourselves and be in a constant state of repentence about sin in the church. If there is sin in our lives we should repent, confess it to God, and seek His forgiveness and strength.

The other question was more personal. Who is sinning? Why do you want to know? Do you want to offer help, strength, and encouragement? This is a worthy motive. Or do you want to know so you can gossip,

Northeastern Baptist School of Ministry
Boston Center Library

crow, and point accusing fingers? This is altogether something else.

Sin is in the church. That is to be expected. After all, the church is a sanctuary for sinners, not a showcase for saints. When we know of our sin, we can claim God's promise: "If we say that we have no sin, we deceive ourselves and there is no truth in us. But if we confess our sins to God, we can trust him, for he does what is right—he will forgive us our sins and make us clean from all our wrongdoing" (I John 1:8-9 TEV).

the high cost of keeping sin out

News releases reported that the Riverside Church in New York City added a $100,000 item to its budget. This expenditure was to provide a new security program for the church.

Due to the growing crime problem in New York City, this church decided to employ eight full-time and four part-time security guards to maintain a twenty-four-hour watch at the church. They were also to make hourly rounds of the building, accompany staff members to the bank, and escort people walking to their apartment buildings after evening services. The church is located in a high crime area, and crimes of all descriptions have occurred near the church.

One hundred thousand dollars! That is a lot of money. That represents a high cost to keep sin out of the church.

Although most churches do not spend that much money to keep sin out, most of us have been caught by the high cost of keeping sin out.

In the church we talk about ideals. And sometimes when we describe what Christians ought to be and could be we make it sound like we are all already there. We know that we aren't. But it might make people who are not Christians think we are. They are honest enough

.... School of Ministry
..on Center Library

to admit they aren't like that. So they would feel uncomfortable in a church, and therefore they don't come.

Church people sometimes get smug in their attitudes. The smugness repels rather than attracts those people who may need the healing power of Christ's gospel. This is part of the high cost of keeping sin out.

There are times when church people have become critical and judgmental. The critical atmosphere toward those who are known transgressors may force them away from the church.

For many reasons, churches have paid the high cost of keeping sin out. And as a result you might be hard put to find a real, honest sinner in the Sunday morning congregation.

Archbishop William Temple once made a remark to the effect that the church exists for those who never come to it. This is a sad fact, when we realize that Jesus was known as the friend of sinners.

Of course, the church must not condone sin. Jesus didn't. But neither should we condemn the sinner to the extent that we never see him again inside the church. He needs Christ and the church, and forgiveness. We, too, need Christ and the church and forgiveness. We must make sure that we have not paid too high a price to keep sin out.

what is condemned?

A few years ago the news headlines announced the damage to churches from the California earthquake. In the *Baptist Standard*, the Texas Baptist paper, the headline proclaimed: "2 Baptist Churches condemned, 5 damaged in LA earthquake." An alert reader responded to the headline and gently took the *Standard* to task with the reminder, "Only the meeting houses were condemned . . . not the churches."

This is a reminder we all need. We many times confuse

the church house with the church. The church is the
people. A church is good or bad, condemned or com-
mended, only on the basis of the life, witness, and ministry of the people who are that church.

Many churches have been "condemned" in recent
days. In some circles a favorite indoor sport is condemn-
ing the churches. Churches are condemned for their
identification with the world, their alliance with culture,
their silence on social issues, and their reluctance to
change or innovate.

Honestly now, some of the criticism is justified. Admit-
tedly, there are many ways that churches have not lived
up either to their potential or their purpose. But much
of this criticism is insincere or merely carping. Some
of it is based on misunderstanding and misinformation.

At the same time, much that is positive could be said
about the churches. We perhaps have been silent when
we should have been shouting. Think of the lives
changed, the homes saved, the directions given, and
the good done through the churches.

Countless churches have been condemned and many
more have been damaged. But please get it straight.
When you hear criticism of the church house or of a
church member, or of a church group, or of the church,
then counter the criticism with the commendation.

how do you locate the church?

For many years Dr. Halford Luccock, who was a pro-
fessor of preaching at Yale Divinity School, wrote a satiri-
cal column in the *Christian Century*. The church about
which he centered his article was called "St. John's-
by-the-Gas-Station."

Well, how do you locate a church? Some churches are
located by their geographical location. St. Giles-by-the-
Sea is a famous English church. I always liked St.

Luke's-in-the-Meadow (really, it is a prairie) in Fort Worth, Texas. Baptist churches by the hundreds are named Clear Creek . . . Pine Grove . . . or Crossroads. . . .

Churches are sometimes located by the community name. Other churches are identified by Biblical names like Pisgah, Zion, or Calvary; or by names given to the Savior, such as Emmanuel; or by theological concepts, such as Trinity. Quite often churches are located historically. Every city has its First Baptist Church; it was the first one there.

But have you ever considered locating a church by its function? Could a church be identified by its love, by its outreach, by its compassion, by its ministry?

I don't really care much for the slogans that churches put on their advertising and stationery. But what would be wrong by being known as the Church of the Praying People? Or the Church of the Compassionate Ones? Or the Church of the Ministering Members? Or the Church of Loving Acts?

How do you locate the church? One way to locate the church may be by its proximity to identifiable landmarks. Perhaps a better way to locate the church would be by its function as the people of God.

come prepared to stay

During a revival, a four-year-old girl dressed herself to come to church with her parents. She had on white shoes but insisted on carrying a red purse. Her mother told her that she ought to carry a white purse, but she insisted on the red one.

After they got to church, the girl asked her mother if she wanted to see why she brought her red purse. When she replied that she did, Karen opened the purse and showed her the contents—a nightgown! That girl had come prepared to stay.

When you come to any worship service you, too, should come prepared to stay. Some people are present physically, but they are somewhere else mentally and emotionally throughout the entire service. They came, but they did not come to stay.

Other people may hear the words spoken, but they always apply the truths to "others." They feel the words are just what "others" ought to hear. These people came, but they did not come to stay.

There are folks who simply do not pay attention to what is happening. They refuse to be moved by the songs, inspired by the prayers, spoken to by the Scripture, helped by the sermon, or really involved in the service. They came, but they did not come to stay.

And then there are always those who come, who listen, and who participate in every part of the service, but then they promptly forget it after the service. It was all so familiar, so expected, that they really didn't let it soak in. They came, but they didn't come to stay.

We have heard the Word of God proclaimed. We have been thrilled by soul-stirring music. We have reached heaven through our prayers. Please, when you come to church, come prepared to stay.

answer me!

When my daughter, Chyrisse, was about seven years old she had a disconcerting little trick. She would first ask one of the countless questions that only a seven-year-old girl can ask. Then before you could figure out some kind of an answer, and, at the same time, make sure you had all the possibilities covered, she would demand, "Answer me!"

"Answer me!" This is an incessant demand these days. Why are you a Christian? Why do you hold to the Christian faith? Someone is always demanding, "Answer me!" Long ago Simon Peter told us, "Be ready at all times to answer anyone who asks you to explain the hope you have in you" (I Peter 3:15 TEV).

The young people are demanding that we give them some answers these days. They want to know why people who cheat on income taxes disapprove of cheating on exams; why people who depend on alcoholic beverages to get them through the day are upset by drugs; why people who support churches act unchristian; why social problems, which all admit can't be solved today, are so numerous; why people have to dirty up, litter up, and pollute our land and atmosphere. "Answer me!" is their cry in confrontation after confrontation.

The Christian, of all people, ought to be able to give reason for his actions. The Christian and his church ought to be open to questions. If we stifle questions and cut off debate and refuse dialogue we will never be able adequately to express our Christian faith. And if we do that, we may some time long to hear again the voice of the young people saying, "Answer me!" We must have the kind of openness and honesty that will allow people to ask questions.

"Answer me!" Can you do it? Can you give an answer for your faith, or for your behavior?

"the hottest brand going"

One of our church members came into the church office chuckling to himself. When questioned about the cause of his amusement, he explained that he had a great idea concerning the Conoco station next door that our church had just purchased for expansion purposes. He thought that as Conoco was removing their pumps, grease racks, and signs, they should let our church keep one sign, to be later placed under the First Baptist Church sign. The whole thing would then read, "First Baptist Church—The Hottest Brand Going."

That wouldn't be too bad, would it?

It would be good for the First Baptist Church to be known as the hottest brand of Christian faith in town. To have the fire of compassion burn steadily in the hearts of its people would be a good reputation for any church to have. To have a passion for God and His will would cause the church to make a powerful impact. Wouldn't it be great if throughout our area it was known that the people of the First Baptist Church were on fire for God? Resulting from this would be the witness, the ministry, and the compassionate concern that would help us to be truly God's people at work for Him.

Or if you are not much on the "hottest brand" idea, what about retaining just the word "Going"? The sign would then read, "The First Baptist Church—Going." That would be a Biblical concept. It would imply that we are not content to stay where we are. We want to go. We want to go out in Christian witness. We want to go forward in Christian growth. We want to go onward in the knowing and doing of God's will.

How about it? "First Baptist Church—The Hottest Brand Going." It does have something to commend it, doesn't it?

part six

ABOUT CHRISTIAN CHARACTER

who is responsible?

Billy was in the four-year-old group in his church kindergarten. This little fellow was a terror in his behavior. He pushed the other children, knocked them down,.tripped them, and generally kept things upset. But one day, when they called on him to pray, he said in his prayer, "And Lord, please help those little children not to fall down so much."

That was a masterful request! In one statement he had absolved himself of all responsibility for the other children "falling down" and getting hurt.

We all try to do that. By whatever method we can, we try to escape the responsibility for our actions.

Sometimes we blame it on circumstances.

At other times we are sure that someone else made us act like that.

Or we are convinced that we are the victims of some cosmic conspiracy.

Also, pressures get a lot of the blame these days.

In every way we can think of, we try to get around facing up to the situation and admitting: "I failed" or "I did wrong" or "It was all my fault."

The Bible says a lot about repentance. But a step that precedes repentance is the acceptance of responsibility. We never will repent until we can say, "I am responsible for my actions."

Don't evade responsibility. Accept it. Then you can go on from there in straightening out your life.

how do you like the way you look?

The First Baptist Church sponsored a "Funday" each Thursday through the summer for primary and junior children. They played games, watched films, made things, and generally enjoyed themselves for three hours each week.

One of their last projects was a craft activity in which each child was to cut a silhouette of himself out of black construction paper.

Keith's profile did not look like he thought it should. So he just altered it a little bit here and there. Of course, it did not look like him at all when he had finished with it, but it pleased him.

Isn't that just like us? How many times have we been somewhat displeased with the face we present to the public?

Sometimes we try to alter our appearance to suit us better. Maybe we wear a neat little mask. Perhaps we cover up here and there. There are times when we have outright lied about ourselves. But no matter how much we try to alter our appearance or change our profile the real person is still there.

The only way we can change how we look on the outside is by what we are on the inside. Our attitudes, feelings, and faith show up in the way we look, in what we show the world.

Abraham Lincoln is reported to have remarked that any grown man is responsible for the way he looks.

Some things—hatreds, grudges, disagreements, disagreeable attitudes—make us look bad. Other things kindness, love, gentleness, faith—make us look good.

Do you like the way you look? There is only one way to change it. How about it?

the danger of generalities

Several years ago, the eight-year-old son of a Methodist minister came over to spend the night with an eight-year-old Baptist "P.K."

During the evening meal John (the Methodist "P.K.") and Keith (the Baptist "P.K.") ate together at a smaller table in the kitchen. Observing Keith eat, John said, "I'll tell you one thing—Baptists eat faster than Methodists." A little later in the meal he added, "I can tell that Baptists eat more than Methodists, too."

These two statements are what we call generalities. In the case of the particular Baptist and Methodist in question, John and Keith, the statements were true. That particular Baptist ate both faster and more than did that particular Methodist. But when you take that particular incident and from it make a generalization concerning all Baptists and Methodists, the comparison falls apart.

That is the danger with generalities. They never do hold true all the way across the board. What may be true about one may not be true about everyone.

We fall into this trap many times. We make generalities about professions: "You better watch those lawyers," someone will say. Generalities are made about nationalities: "Now isn't that just like a German," someone may remark. Generalities are made about religious beliefs. Dangerous generalities are made about races of people. Politicians have felt the sting of generalities. Also, preachers have been hurt by stereotyped generalities.

The danger of generalities is that they are never true of everyone in any particular grouping of human beings. What is said may be true of one person, but do not make the mistake of applying it to all the people of a particular category.

how about crossing out failure?

On display in the Dargan-Carver Library at the Baptist Sunday School Board Building in Nashville, Tennessee, is the dictionary, which belonged to B. W. Spilman, with the word "failure" crossed out.

Elected in 1896 as the first Sunday school missionary for North Carolina, Spilman was told in 1897 that his program for teaching and training Baptists in North Carolina could not succeed.

After hours of prayer concerning this matter to which he had given his life, Spilman reached for his desk dictionary and marked out the word "failure." Failure did not exist for Spilman after that day.

What would happen if more people would cross out failure?

One of the biggest hindrances people face is the fear of failure. There is no telling how many worthwhile and promising ventures were never started simply because the persons involved were afraid of failure.

Some marriages have failed simply because the people were too willing to admit failure.

There are needed acts of ministry that were never performed because someone was afraid of being re-buffed—they feared failure.

Some fine Christian people have never taught Sunday school classes, led training groups, or counseled young people, simply because they were afraid that they might fail.

Many needed words of Christian witness have gone undelivered because someone was afraid that he could not win that soul, and thus fail.

Some folks have never trusted Christ and stepped out in faith because they were afraid that they wouldn't hold out, and thus fail.

How about crossing out failure in your life? You will be much richer for it.

how do you build
something that lasts?

In this mechanical and technical age in which we live, we have some of the finest gadgets imaginable. We can do mechanically almost anything that needs to be done. But how do you build something that lasts?

I don't know how it is at your house, but there are times at our house when it seems that almost everything that's supposed to work doesn't. There are breakdowns. Parts wear out. How do you build something that lasts?

Then add style changes, and you really run into trouble. Vance Packard says that American industry is committed to "planned obsolescence." It is no accident that your appliances are soon out of date. They were designed to be. How do you build something that lasts?

Probably you cannot build gadgets, machines, or appliances that last. But you can build a life that lasts.

You begin by trusting your life to Jesus Christ and to His care. You continue by living a life of continual faith. Then you try to develop Christian character as an integral part of your life.

Christian character is developed by church attendance, Bible study, prayer, and conscious imitation of the life of Christ. Many activities that we enter into at church help to build Christian character: Sunday school, mission organizations, music activities, Vacation Bible School.

You will not be able to build anything except your life that can last for all eternity. Since this is true, don't you think you ought to give a lot more of your attention to building that life? This week is a good time to start.

working hard . . .
for the wrong things

I guess it happens sometime in the career of every athlete.

Craig is on the seventh-grade basketball team at his junior high school. They won a hard-fought game against an opposing junior high school by just two points.

When the second half began, Craig's team was behind. The opposing team got the tip-off, but the boy fumbled the ball and Craig grabbed it away from him, took off dribbling like mad down the court, and amid the screams of the crowd executed a perfect lay-up shot—in the wrong basket!

He had worked hard. But it was for the wrong goal. The opposing team got two points.

A lot of us work hard for the wrong things. Jesus chided His followers one time for not being as imaginative and hard working and dedicated as the "sons of darkness." People often use a lot more energy, effort, and imagination in working for every other cause under the sun than in service for Christ.

Think what it could mean to the church if as much effort were put into church activities as is put into clubs and civic organizations.

Think how well the cause of Christ could be presented if as much money were spent in its activities as is spent in radio and television advertising.

Think of all the imagination that is used in promoting new products; then project that kind of imaginative thinking into ways of presenting the gospel to a sated world.

We are working hard, all right. But sometimes we work for the wrong goal. Direct some of your energy, efforts, and imagination to service for Christ. It will pay dividends.

there's always an alternative

Tynes Hildebrand, head basketball coach at Northwestern State University, tells an interesting church story.

While on a recruiting trip in central Louisiana he came across a church with a sign in front of it. Since he is a deacon he was interested in what the sign said. In addition to the normal information—church name, pastor's name, and time of services—it also had a message. The message was: "All you that are tired of sin come on in." Underneath that, scribbled in lipstick, were the words "All you that ain't call 2242."

There's always an alternative. Every time you have an opportunity to rid yourself of sin, to receive God's forgiveness, and to find strength and renewal, there is also an opportunity to stay right where you are.

Temptation is ever present. The forces of evil are constantly at work. With every invitation to come to God there is also an opportunity to choose to sin.

The possibility of choice is what makes us human. God created us as free moral agents. He does not force His will upon us. He does not make us find forgiveness. He does not force us to accept Christ. We make the choice; the decision is ours.

It is with God's strength and guidance that we are able to make the right choices. When we grow weary with our sin, when we feel the need of forgiveness, when we realize our own strength is gone, we can go into the presence of God and receive strength, forgiveness, and grace.

But there always is an alternative. Nonetheless, God's grace is present when we choose to come to Him.

hope for humans

In Bournemouth, England, a dishwashing machine manufacturer challenged any housewife to match her dishwashing ability against his machine.

A forty-nine-year-old housewife accepted the challenge. During the course of the three-course dinner, which included coffee and liqueurs, many dishes were dirtied. The dirty dishes were then divided equally between the dishwashing machine and the dishwashing housewife. The contest began.

The housewife won! She washed her dishes in twenty-one minutes and fifty-two seconds. The machine took an hour. Not only that, a panel of three judges decided that her dishes were cleaner than the machine's.

The crowd (which had been gathered by the manufacturer) cheered. The housewife was quoted to say, "I felt great to have beaten the machine."

So there is hope for humans after all.

In the depersonalization of our age, we often feel that our lives are almost completely dominated by machines. We seem to be at the mercy of computers, labor-saving devices, and household appliances. Let a power failure occur and we realize how helpless we are in this machine age.

But the Bible stresses the importance of persons. In the face of depersonalization, our spiritual heritage highlights personalization.

God became a person in Jesus Christ. God ministers to us as persons. Jesus said that the very hairs of our heads are numbered, which means, among other things, that each of us is important. We receive Christ as Savior personally.

There is hope for humans. We have not been replaced by machines. Nor do we have to be dominated by machines. We still have the assurance that we are significant and important as individuals.

"on a clear day you can see forever"

One of the outstanding attractions in Saint Louis, Missouri, is the Gateway Arch. Completed in 1965, the arch is well over 600 feet high. The observation area itself is over 630 feet. It symbolizes St. Louis as the "Gateway to the West" in the days of American western expansion and settlement.

You must not fail to go up into the Gateway Arch when you get to St. Louis. The ascent is made in a series of little capsule-type elevator cars that adjust periodically so that you are always sitting straight up. The guide explains that on a clear day you can see twenty-five to thirty miles, both east into Illinois and west into Missouri.

This perhaps makes you think of the Broadway musical, which was later made into a movie, "On a Clear Day You Can See Forever." The story is not important. But the title is intriguing: "On a Clear Day You Can See Forever."

There are times when we need a vision so clear that we can look down the corridor of time into forever. There are occasions when we need to look past time into eternity. In each of our lives, at various times, we need a vision so clear that we can see forever.

An obvious time, of course, is when we consider our relationship to Jesus Christ. On that day we need to see forever. We must understand that our acceptance of Jesus Christ determines our eternal destiny. After this life is over there is no further opportunity to decide.

In the times of temptation, when a moral judgment must be made and made quickly, we need to be able to see forever. How many people have ruined their lives because they have failed to look at the possible, or even probable, consequences of an act?

When you chart the direction that your life will take and establish its patterns and habits, you need to be able to see clearly into forever. What you build as a life now is what you will have to live with forever.

a machine we could all use

An interesting advertisement appeared in the Shreveport *Times*. Among many ordinary items listed for sale was one that was very unusual—a "coping machine."

Obviously it was a typographical error. The machine was really a copying machine.

Think of the number of times that you would have been able to use a coping machine. So many times life places situations before us with which we can hardly cope. A coping machine would surely come in handy then.

For instance, parents are sometimes called upon to cope with situations with their children that strain parental understanding and patience. How can they strike the proper balance between freedom and control? How can they give the needed independence without turning them loose on their own? How a coping machine would help!

Sickness, disease, accidents, and death place demands on humans that sometimes seem to be more than can be successfully borne. Many of these situations could be aided by a coping machine.

And what about those times when you are irritated, aggravated, worried, or just plain "bugged" by something or someone. Wouldn't a coping machine help then?

Yes, a coping machine would help. We think. But would it really? By having to cope with demanding situations we build character, create integrity, and learn to trust in God.

There was a time when the people of Judah formed an alliance with Egypt against Assyria. Egypt had horses and chariots. To the threatened Judeans this was the finest coping machine they knew. But the prophet Isaiah reminded them: "The Egyptians are men, and not God; and their horses are flesh, and not spirit. When the Lord stretches out his hand, the helper will stumble, and he who is helped will fall, and they will all perish together" (Isa. 31:3 RSV).

Need a coping machine? We have one, the finest made—faith in God. We just need to use it.

part seven

ABOUT
CHRISTIAN
WITNESS

principles for personal proclamation

If you are a fisherman, you will be interested in the book written by Grits Gresham entitled *The Complete Book of Bass Fishing*. Of all the helpful material in that book, three principles stand out. For successful bass fishing you need to locate the fish, use the right lure, and practice the craft.

Jesus told us that we ought to be "fishers of men." While respecting the rights and dignity of human personality, I think that Grits Gresham's three principles certainly can be used to good advantage in personal witnessing for Christ.

First, you need to know where to locate the persons who need Christ. These really are not hard to find. All around us are people with deep personal needs to whom we can give a word of positive witness.

Second, you need to know how to attract people to Christ by using an effective "lure." People have used all kinds of lures to bring others to Christ. Frankly, some have acted on less than the highest motives and have used methods not in keeping with their high purpose. It is the Holy Spirit of God who convicts people of sin and draws them to Christ. The real "lure" is the deep human need for forgiveness and new life. The Spirit of Christ convinces of this.

Third, we must practice. Personal witnessing is really more than a craft to practice; it is an experience that we share. Of course, you might not be satisfied with your first efforts and presentations. Practice. Find others who need to know of Christ and salvation, of forgiveness and fulfillment, and share the good news of Christ.

show and tell!
the purpose of witness

One of the most potentially hazardous undertakings in teaching kindergarten, first, or second grade is the "Show and Tell" activity. Almost universally, teachers who moderate these sessions adopt the slogan, "Always expect the unexpected."

One elementary schoolgirl, after her daddy and older brother each had shot a deer, excitedly asked if she could take the two deer heads to school for "Show and Tell." Imagine a petite girl laboriously dragging the two hunting trophies into her classroom and her teacher slipping to the floor from her chair in a fainting spell. Of course, the girl's ambitious request was denied.

But, "Show and Tell" is a good concept. In fact, it is an excellent description of Christian witness.

The Christian witness is to show by his life what it means to be a Christian. He may need to show how Christians react to sorrow and suffering. He may need to show how a Christian takes discouragements or disappointments. He may need to show kindness, gentleness, love, and grace in his dealings with other people. He may need to show how to have positive concepts in the midst of a negative atmosphere. He may need to show how a person can be clean and honest in his life when others around him are dirty and cheating.

But after he has shown all this, the Christian witness also should tell why it is possible. If you never get around to giving a verbal witness you could live a Christian life for a lifetime and no one would ever know your secret—your faith and commitment to Jesus Christ.

There comes a time when you have to tell, "Christ has changed my life."

"Show and Tell"—it's a good idea. It is a very good description of Christian witnessing.

when you drop the hot potato

During the course of discussion at a seminar on Christian witnessing, the leader, Alan Richardson, described the gospel as "hot potato news." Then the leader attempted to explain the quotation. He said, "Suppose you were out camping and had cooked your meal over an open fire. Someone reached in the coals and pulled out a potato wrapped in aluminum foil and tossed it to you. What would you do?" Very quickly a girl sitting on the front row said, "I would drop it."

She surely ruined that illustration! What the leader was driving at was that one doesn't just stand around holding a hot potato. He passes it on—he does something with it. In one sense that girl's illustration was better than his. "Dropping the hot potato" happens too often.

Christians have been given that kind of news: it is "hot" news; it is the kind of news that needs to be passed on. But what have many done? They have dropped it. In "Tell It Like It Is" young people sing:

> It only takes a spark to get a fire going.
> And soon all those around can warm up in
>   its glowing.
> That's how it is with God's love.
> Once you've experienced it, you spread His
>   love to ev'ryone;
> You want to pass it on.
> I'll shout it from the mountain top,
> I want my world to know,
> The Lord of love has come to me,
> I want to pass it on.

PASS IT ON by Kurt Kaiser

From the musical, TELL IT LIKE IT IS © Copyright 1969 by LEXICON MUSIC, INC. All Rights Reserved. International Copyright Secured. Used by Special Permission. Performance rights licensed through ASCAP.

When you receive the Good News, the "hot potato news," the gospel, don't just stand there and drop it. Pass it on.

the difference between loving and liking

Not long ago a pastor spoke at a youth retreat for another church. After the message, one evening, they had a dialogue session, a talk-back.

One of the young people asked the pastor to define "love" as he had used it in the message. He said, "Well, to begin with, we are talking about loving, not liking. There is a difference between loving a person in the Christian sense and liking that person. You can love them without liking them."

One girl retorted, "But that doesn't sound right. How could you love someone enough to marry him without liking him?"

The leader's reply was that they were not discussing romantic love, the marrying kind; they were discussing Christian love, the ministering kind.

Then all of a sudden one teen-age girl came alive. She had a light of revelation on her face, and she almost jumped out of her chair. "You know," she said, "it's like you love your parents."

And with this insight the distinction became clear to these young people. Teen-agers can love their parents without liking them.

The word "love" covers a multitude of attitudes and actions. God requires that we love one another because He has loved us and we love Him. Jesus said that the first commandment is that we love God supremely. The second greatest commandment is related: we are to love our neighbors as ourselves. Jesus indicated that people would know we were His disciples by the quality of our love. John, in his First Epistle, equates love with keeping the commandments of God. James called love "the royal law."

We often have been hesitant to love because we didn't like. That is our distinction, not God's. God calls on us to act in loving, ministering ways whether we like the object of the loving act or not. There is a distinction between loving and liking.

how you grow tall . . .
and how you have revival

Craig received an interesting advertisement recently from an outfit named New Height in Ontario, Canada. In it was a pamphlet entitled "How To Be Taller." Supposedly it is a method to increase basal metabolism to stimulate bone and ligament growth and to increase the cartilage area between the discs of the spinal column.

Since Craig wasn't the tallest guy in town, he was somewhat interested in it. For the moment he forgot that artificial methods, even those that are supposed to stimulate body growth, don't make you grow taller. No matter what the advertisements claim, your height will not be increased above normal growth.

Neither do you have a revival simply by announcing one. You can enlist an outstanding preacher; you can bring in a fine singer; you can set dates; you can schedule services; you can arrange for special activities, and still not have a revival.

Revival comes when the people of God turn to God in repentance and faith. Revival comes when Christians earnestly pray for revival. Revival comes when concerned believers will visit, witness to, and bring unbelievers with them to the services. Revival comes when church members become committed to and burdened for the revival. But in the end, revival comes when God blesses the efforts and people respond to His presence and hearts are made right with God.

The following verse was not originally referring to a revival in the sense of a protracted meeting, but it does tell about revival as a blessing from God. Listen again: "If my people, who are called by my name, shall humble themselves, and pray, and seek my face, and turn from their wicked ways; then will I hear from heaven, and will forgive their sin, and heal their land" (II Chron. 7:14 ASV).

There are some ways in which people try to grow taller that do not really work. And there are some ways that people try to have revival that do not really work. Try God's way.

how to write right

Sure enough, there it was, just as it had been reported. Stuck in the front window at Gibson's was a sign proclaiming: "Here Jim Elliff Tell It Like It Is — First Baptist Church."

The young people had made and distributed the signs announcing the youth revival. Apparently, someone had trouble distinguishing between "here" and "hear." Of course, they may have meant "Hear Jim Elliff here" or they could have had in mind "Here Jim Elliff will tell it like it is."

There is always the outside possibility that "here" was used instead of "hear" as an attention-getting device. But anyway, there it was as big as life: "Here Jim Elliff Tell It Like It Is — First Baptist Church."

There is one thing significant about all this: whoever made that sign didn't use the right word in the right place—but he did make a sign! There are some of us who are so afraid of not doing something correctly that we never do anything. But, really, performance is more important than perfection. If most of us waited until we were able to do anything perfectly we would never get it done.

Of course, it would be better to write right. But it is better to write with a small mistake than not to write at all. It might even be better to have a hand-lettered sign in imperfect English rather than a commercially printed sign into which no one had put anything of himself.

I think of the lady who counted the grammatical errors in one of Dwight L. Moody's sermons. After the service, she told him how many grammatical errors he had made that night. He replied that he was sorry but that he was serving the Lord to the best of his ability. Was she?

Don't fail to serve God because you are afraid you will make a mistake. Dare to fail along with the rest of us. Use whatever abilities you have for our Savior.

what it's all about
in christian witnessing

Mobil Oil Company has an interesting safety slogan: "We want you to live." It is printed blue on a white background on circles with an adhesive on the back. These are stuck on metal hats, on envelopes, on walls, and on bulletin boards. The message is made plain: "We want you to live."

That also is the burden of Christian witnessing. That is the message the Christian witness is trying to get across to other people: "We want you to live."

There are a lot of people who are alive but do not live. As Christians we believe that life, real life, comes only through faith in Jesus Christ. He has promised us that life. And He delivers what He promises.

Our responsibility is to get that message across to others. We want others to live. We want them to know the peace, the joy, and the meaning that comes with new life in Christ.

That is what it's all about in Christian witnessing: telling others that we want them to live. Many are the ways we can do it. Concern for them and obedience to God in being a witness wherever we are is how we go about it.

"We want you to live." That's what it is all about in Christian witnessing. Let's get the message across.

people are all much alike

I spotted her in Amsterdam. She was a little chubby-legged, rosy-cheeked girl of about six to eight years of age skipping along by a frozen canal. With a book satchel in her hand she obviously was skipping happily toward home from school.

I saw another one in Jerusalem. A little dark-haired, dark-eyed, bronze-skinned girl of about the same age. Clutching books in her arms she was skipping along—obviously on her way home from school.

Back in Natchitoches I watched Chyrisse, our little blond-headed, longer legged, and slightly chubby seven-year-old school girl skip down the driveway after school one day.

People are all much alike. Little school girls skip happily home from school whether they are Dutch, Israeli, or American.

We all, then, have some of the same needs. When the Bible says that "*all* have sinned and come short of the glory of God" it recognizes the common need of the forgiveness of sin shared by all of us.

Acceptance is a need that we all have. Those who are supposed to know tell us that many of the things people do are done not particularly because they want to do them but that they might be accepted by a group, by a person, or by persons.

We need the warmth and security of love. Each person

desperately searches for someone who loves him as he is, "warts and all."

People are all much alike. Wherever you find people you find those who need forgiveness, acceptance, and love.

You know what? All of these basic needs are met in Jesus Christ, He is the only one who provides forgiveness of sin, accepts us, and loves us even when we may not be too loveable. Even though we have some common characteristics, we are each individual persons. And that is how Jesus reaches us—as individuals.

getting what you want

Things had gotten to be a little tough financially for one father. One of his boys was in college at the time. So Dad decided he would sell his farm in Arkansas. That would give him the breathing room he needed.

He wrote the advertisement to be put in the paper. After he had written the advertisement he read it to his wife. He had stated the acreage, described the amount in cultivation, told about the pasture and praised the timber. The house on it was mentioned and its location stated. Then he read the advertisement again. After this, he remarked to her: "You know, that sounds just exactly like the farm I have always wanted. I think I ought to keep it." And he tore up the advertisement.

What kind of life do you really want? If you were able to list the elements in a life that would be full, rich, and meaningful, what would you include?

Likely you would say that you would want a purpose for your life, meaning in your life, love, acceptance, and security.

Do you know what? That kind of life is exactly what we have in Jesus Christ. Jesus said, "I came that they might have life." He promised life in all its fullness, meaning, and purpose. He gives you love, acceptance, and security.

G. K. Chesterton once made this interesting comparison. He likened the people who had left the church in a search for a more meaningful existence to a group of Englishmen who set out to discover a new area. They sailed for days and then sighted land. Upon reaching the land and exploring it they decided that it was exactly what they wanted. They liked the climate, approved of the terrain, and felt comfortable on its shores. So they ran up their flag and claimed it. Then they discovered that they had simply sailed around the island and had landed again on England—their home.

Wherever you search, you cannot find life more meaningful than new life in Christ. Set out your specifications. Then look again at Christ. Then claim Him again as your Savior. This is getting what you want.

suppose he were your brother

Perhaps you have seen these billboards. They picture a rather forlorn figure, with shaved head and dressed in a pajama type suit, sitting on a stool. The caption reads: "Suppose this POW were your brother. . . . Well, he is."

In a moving manner this proclaims a truth we sometimes want to forget: We are all related to one another; we have a responsibility to one another.

We often try to ignore that. We order our affairs as though we were the only ones to be considered. We tend to keep from getting involved with others, their lives, and their problems.

It was a long time ago that Cain asked the Lord, "Am I my brother's keeper?" In a very real way, we are our brother's keeper. We have a responsibility toward him. When he is loveless we are to love him. When he is hurt we are to help him. When he is hopeless we are to encourage him. When he is weak we are to strengthen him. When he is lost we are to guide him. When he stumbles we are to uphold him.

Sometime ago a plan was devised to inoculate people in undeveloped countries by using a gun to give shots. That project was developed by a Baptist physician. First they called it "Operation Brother's Keeper"; then they changed the name to "Operation Brother's Brother." That, I think, is much more suggestive. Rather than being just my brother's keeper, I am my brother's brother.

Suppose this man were your brother. Well, he is. And because of it you need to share God's love with him and to show real concern for him.

part eight

ABOUT CHRISTIAN PRAYER

confidence in prayer

A little five-year-old girl was sitting on her mother's lap after Sunday lunch. Her mother found a gray hair in her very brunette head. Her paternal grandmother then commented that it would not be strange for her to have gray hair early since her maternal grandmother was prematurely gray. This brought on a discussion about gray hair.

While the adults were discussing the subject the little girl bowed her head and was almost through with her prayer before the adults realized she was praying. She prayed, "Dear Lord, please don't let me be gray-headed when I am five years old."

Then without further ado, she slipped off her mother's lap and went outside to play.

That is confidence in prayer.

When the prayer was completed, the matter was settled as far as she was concerned. There was no use worrying about it any more or discussing it any more. It was now in the hands of the Lord.

Jesus taught us to pray with confidence. But how often do we pray with absolute confidence? Too many times we pray to hand an item of concern over to the Lord, but then we continue to be concerned about it, worried over it, and bugged by it.

Confident prayer realizes that God can handle any situation we place in His hands. When you pray, have confidence that God will hear, handle, and answer your prayer. God is worthy of such confidence.

prayer for the common things

Our family had a fine little feisty puppy who had the very descriptive but absolutely unimaginative name of "Puppy." He fell ill with a disease peculiar to dogs that just could not be cured, so Puppy was given away.

Then we got a new puppy. This one was a brown and white spotted fox terrier that was born bob-tailed. He was given the name "Punkin Puppy."

On the night that we got him, the children prayed as usual before going to bed. Our eight-year-old son prayed, "Lord, bless our new puppy and please don't let him get sick with the mange or anything else, and, Lord, please bless Puppy [our other puppy that had to be given away] and make him happy wherever he is."

An adult might smile at that prayer. But that boy got to the heart of prayer.

Prayer is expressing to God whatever is a matter of concern to you. If it is important enough to worry you and to concern you, it is important enough to pray about. There are no objects too trivial for prayer.

Too long we have imprisoned prayer in stately phrases, in vague generalities, unfamiliar "Thees" and "Thous" and "dosts," and in other proper forms. Prayer is communion with God. And communion shares all matters of concern.

Those you love most on the earth are concerned about things that concern you. How much time do husbands and wives spend talking about things that to others would seem trivial? If prayer is to be practiced, it must include the common things. Prayer for the common concerns is not blasphemy. It is getting right to the heart of prayer.

things that have to be done again

One Saturday Dad spent all day working in the yard.

From the time he got up until late afternoon he labored. The leaves were swept off the roof. The flower beds were cleaned. The limbs were picked up. Vines were cut down. Trimming was done. It was a full day of labor and he was glad when it was over.

Then during the next week they had two rains. Now they really needed the rain and he was thankful for it.

But do you know what? He had most of his work to do over again. Leaves were on the roof again. Limbs were in the yard again. Flower beds had leaves and weeds in them again.

How often God has the same thing to do with us. You would think that once God has us all cleaned up and forgiven that He could put us on a shelf and say, "Well, now that one is finished. Let me see who I can work on next." But it just does not work that way.

God has to come back again and again to lift us up when we have fallen, to give us guidance in some decision, to forgive us for some sin that we had committed before, to comfort us in some sorrow, and to strengthen us against some temptation we have faced many times already.

And we would be happy if all these problems, sins, temptations, feelings, and pressures could be dealt with once and for all. But it just does not work that way.

And there are some things we have to do again and again. Prayer is one of them. And there is work with us that God has to do again and again. Bishop Gerald Kennedy of the Methodist Church once commented on the experience of the children of Israel in gathering manna every day for that day's use. "We are being told that there are some things we cannot save up for the future, and there are some values which can be neither pickled or embalmed. There in the wilderness, God was teaching the people that the great values of life have to be gathered afresh every morning."

where should concern begin?

Some time ago, Myra Gulledge, BSU Director at Northwestern State University, called me just after lunch. She was very concerned. Aline Fuselier, state YWA Director and a former member of our church, was supposed to leave that day by airplane from Asheville, North Carolina, to return home from Ridgecrest. Myra had just heard on a television newscast that an airliner and a light plane had collided over Hendersonville, North Carolina, near Asheville. Myra was afraid that Aline might have been on that plane.

We got busy and checked schedules and heard more complete news reports and then ascertained that Aline was not on the plane. I left the BSU Center with a feeling of relief.

But then I began to question my feeling of relief. We were relieved because a mutual friend was not killed. But what of those nearly eighty families whose family members were killed? What of the wide circle including all the friends of the people involved in the tragedy?

Where should our concern begin? It often begins —and ends—only close to home. If what the New Testament teaches is true, and I'm convinced that it is, our concern, our interest, and our love should reach out to all men.

Thus, when tragedy strikes, it is not enough for Christians to breathe a sigh of relief and say, "Thank God, there is no riot in Natchitoches . . . none of my family was on the plane . . . my brother was not killed in Viet Nam. . . ." Instead, with Christian concern we should reach out in love and in prayer to all people who have need. Concern should begin wherever men have need.

the sounds of praying

A preacher had been asked to give the invocation

at a football game. He and his two sons found seats and were getting settled when the preacher suddenly realized that the band was lining up on the field for playing the National Anthem. The preacher then realized he was late, and their seats were in the section nearest the playing field on about the twenty-yard line. So he went charging up the stadium steps all the way to the top, dashed through the press box, and got to the announcer just as he was saying, "And now the invocation . . ." and handed the microphone to the preacher.

In all his life he had never sounded so "religious" when he prayed. As he was trying both to catch his breath and to control it, he had the most "religious" quiver in his voice you have ever heard.

That is what some people call the sound of praying. And it has caused some people to wonder about the effectiveness of their praying simply because it doesn't sound "religious" enough.

For praying to be effective it must be sincere. The quiver in the voice doesn't count. Neither do the "Thees, Thous, and hasts" that we usually associate with prayer. They have their place, but they are not absolutely necessary. Nor is there a special structure that the prayer must take in order to be right.

Real prayer is the expression of our needs, the confession of our sins, the voicing of our gratitude, the stating of our petitions, the sharing of our concerns with God.

Paul once made this statement in talking about prayer: "In the same way the Spirit also comes to us, weak that we are. For we do not know how we ought to pray; the Spirit himself pleads with God for us, in groans that words cannot express" (Rom. 8:20 TEV). These, I think, are the real sounds of praying.

when the pros make mistakes

Even pros make mistakes. At the Astrodome, a Houston Astros pitcher threw a terribly wild pitch. In the same game, a third baseman bobbled a simple grounder. It even happens at the Ringling Brothers, Barnum and Bailey Circus, "The Greatest Show on Earth"; a juggler dropped a pin he was juggling. At the professional football games you may have seen a guard miss a block or an end drop a pass. Professional basketball players have been known to miss easy lay-up shots. Doug Sanders lost the British Open Golf Tournament because of a muffed putt.

Even the pros make mistakes. But what do they do when they make a mistake? Watch them. They will go right back out there and execute the same play.

One thing they have learned is that a mistake doesn't have to be final. Sure they dropped one ball, missed one shot, or blew one hole. But that doesn't mean the end of the game. There are other opportunities, and they don't quit the game because they made one mistake.

And what happens when we make a mistake in life? The assurance of grace is that a mistake doesn't have to be final. God gives us other opportunities. With contrition and confession we have the promise of forgiveness and the opportunity to live again, to try again, to serve again.

When the pros make mistakes, they recognize what they have done. They try to correct the error and go out to play again. When a Christian makes a mistake, he should own up to his failure, confess to God, and go on, with the consciousness of forgiveness, to live and to love again.

how to talk to God
when you aren't feeling ridiculous

I had just bought a new book, *How to Talk to God*

When You Aren't Feeling Religious. It was resting on the little table in the bedroom on which the telephone also sits.

Chryisse was talking to one of her friends over the telephone. Her mother heard her tell her friend, "Daddy has the funniest book here. It is called *How to Talk to God When You Aren't Feeling Ridiculous.*"

Well, that really isn't the title of the book. But it might be a pretty good reminder for us.

Many of us have the idea that the only time you talk to God is when you are feeling ridiculous. At those times when you have failed spectacularly and miserably, you feel ridiculous enough to pray. At those times when you obviously need a strength greater than yours and a power beyond your own, you may feel ridiculous enough to pray. At those times when the doors have shut, when the answers won't come, and when there seems no way out, you probably feel ridiculous enough to pray. At those times when you feel that you are absolutely alone, when no other person stands with you or no one else understands you, you might feel ridiculous enough to pray.

That is the way we often do it, isn't it? We don't pray until we get to feeling ridiculous.

But aren't there times when you ought to talk to God when you aren't feeling ridiculous? Surely there are times when you could voice praise to God, express joy in your relationship with Him, share your innermost thoughts with Him, or just enjoy His company in fellowship.

You don't have to feel ridiculous to pray. In fact, some of your greatest adventures in prayer may be at those times when you talk with God when you aren't feeling ridiculous.

who has a straight line?

A pastor from San Antonio told of coming to his office one afternoon to be greeted by a handful of telephone messages.

So he began at the top of the stack and started working his way through them. After returning several calls he came to one that had just the telephone number noted. He dialed that number, and the voice that answered said, "Holy Ghost."

Immediately he thought, "This is what I have always wanted, a straight line to the Holy Ghost." Then he realized that he had reached the Holy Ghost Fathers, a Roman Catholic order in San Antonio.

All of us would like a straight line to God. But who has one? Some people act like they do. They act as if they were the only ones with whom God communicates. They know the will of God and no one else does.

But, really, none of us has such a straight line to God that we have all the answers. God has determined that we find His will only by searching for it, by praying earnestly for it, by using our powers of reasoning, and by opening ourselves to the leadership of the Holy Spirit. This is the hardest way, but it is the best way.

By seeking to find God's will, we develop faith; we develop patience; we develop an openness to God; we develop an awareness of His Spirit and His work.

Jesus said, "Seek, and ye shall find; ask, and it shall be given to you; knock, and it shall be opened to you." This comes only through earnest prayer—not by way of a straight-line hook-up with God.

We don't always know where the will of God will lead us. It sometimes will lead different ones of us in different directions. But until we all receive a straight line to the Holy Ghost, we must seek God's will through earnest prayer—and follow His will as He makes it known to us.

when God speaks

A little girl, about four or five years of age, was afraid to go to bed in the dark by herself. So after she had left her bed several times and had come back into the den, her father had a little talk with her. He explained to her that God was everywhere and that God was in that dark room with her, too. She was not really alone. God was there.

That seemed to satisfy her and she started back down the hall to the bedroom. Just before entering the door she was heard to say, "God, if you are in there, please don't say anything 'cause it would scare me to death."

How many times have we done the same thing? We say that we want to hear God speak—but if He did it would absolutely frighten us to death.

During our services of worship we hope to hear God speak. It probably won't be audibly—that would be too scary for us. But we hope to see the results of God's power at work in the lives of people. We hope to hear God call people to repentance, faith, and salvation. We hope to hear God speak words of encouragement, hope, and healing, to people in need.

God may speak through the minister or the choir, or through your own prayers and preparatory Bible study.

God is everywhere. God is with you now. We believe that He wants us to have a real, spiritual experience with Him. Tune your hearts and ears to hear God when He speaks to you.

when you need God

When a fisherman is late coming in from fishing it means one of two things. Either the fish are biting or they are not biting. If the fish are biting he just cannot leave with all that activity going on. If the fish are not biting he can't afford to leave because they might start biting any minute.

Our need for God is about the same way.

When things are going well, we need God because we recognize that He is the source of all our blessings. We need to thank Him and praise Him for the love He has shown to us.

When things are not going well we surely need God. We need His strength; we need His guidance; we need His comforting presence.

You can consider prayer from the same standpoint. When do you need to pray? All the time. You need to pray when you are aware of the goodness of God. And you need to pray when you are in the depths of despair or in a tight place. You need to pray when things are going well and when things are not going well.

And what about worship? The same principle applies. Why turn to God in worship only in times of crisis? You need the confrontation by God and the communion with God every day of your life. I am reminded of a woman who prayed during a storm. Afterward she demanded to know why God didn't answer her prayer. The wise counselor to whom she was talking replied, "I don't know, unless He was busy waiting on His regular customers."

You really don't know when you will need God. Things can go from good to bad very quickly. The truth is that you need God at all times. So when you feel the need for the presence of God, for praying to God, and for worshiping God, it means that things are either going well or not so well. You need God at all times.

when the instructions come from above

An assistant district attorney told me this "preacher story."

A minister had been stopped by a highway patrolman for speeding. The clergyman protested, but the patrolman convinced him that there was no argument: they had the goods on him; he was speeding.

Then he asked the office how they knew that he was speeding. He replied that he had been clocked by a traffic helicopter.

"Well," answered the preacher with a tone of resignation, "I always listen to instructions from above."

Wouldn't it be great if we all were that definite about listening to instructions from above?

Our basic problem is knowing whether the instructions come from above or from within, whether they are God's will or our desires.

Most of us have never heard God speak audibly. Wouldn't it be something special if we got all of our instructions from God out loud? But then that would remove the element of faith from following God's will.

Sometimes the instructions do come from above. In a time of prayer we get a definite impression that something should be done.

Or maybe it is not a sudden inspiration but rather an increasing awareness. Over a period of time we may think about something, brood over it, mull it over in the back of our mind, or maybe just let it simmer on the back burner of the brain. At any rate, we somehow come to realize that there is something specific that we should do.

There are times when the will of God comes from within. Because of a basic commitment to God, a person moves to a particular decision. In his heart he knows that this is right.

But we never remove the element of faith from following the will of God. Often it is only in retrospect that we are convinced that what we have done was God's will for us. At the time, however, it was carried out with fear and trembling. But when viewing it later from the perspective of faith we know that it was right.

Seeking to find and follow God's will may be somewhat difficult at times. But that is our great quest as Christians.

part nine

ABOUT
CHRISTIAN
CONCERNS

what kind of creature are you?

A little boy was brought to a worship service in a large church building for the first time. Excited about where he was, he kept asking questions, making comments, or just chattering. His parents kept trying to quiet him by saying, "Be quiet. The preacher will be here in just a minute"; or, "Now you will have to be quiet when the preacher comes in."

After a while the preacher came in. The deacons came in, the choir came in, and the preacher stepped up to the platform. Just as he reached the platform, the child asked in a stage whisper, "Is that the creature?"

Well, there may be times when a preacher feels more like a creature than a preacher. And no doubt there are times when you, too, wonder what kind of creature you are.

One time a shepherd psalmist stepped out into the night, looked up at the stars and said, "Lord, our Lord, your greatness is seen in all the world! . . . When I look at the moon and stars, which you have set in their places—what is man, that you think of him; mere man, that you care for him?" (Ps. 8:1, 3-4 TEV).

What kind of creature are you? God made you as the supreme creature of all creation. Man was the crown of creation.

But you have to balance this majestic concept of man with what you have made of yourself. You are also a sinning creature. By choice all of us have become sinners.

But that is not all there is to it. You can be a saved

creature. Christ has died on the cross to give you salvation. By believing on Him you can be a saved creature.

A Scotsman once prayed, or thought he was praying, against all the forces that crush one's life, "O Lord, help me to have a high opinion of myself."

Here comes the creature! But what kind of creature are you? Claim God's grace to be the kind of creature who can have a high opinion of himself by being certain that God loves him through Jesus Christ.

an imitation of an imitation

Has your wife ever come home from the grocery store with dietary margarine? If so, you perhaps noticed that on the lid it was labeled as "imitation margarine." Then you also remembered that margarine is imitation butter. So if you use dietary margarine, just keep in mind that you are using an imitation of an imitation!

But that happens in our Christian life, too. You might decide that you will pattern your life after someone you admire as a Christian. However, you should remember that in doing that, at best you are an imitation of an imitation because he probably has patterned his life after someone else.

To the Philippian Christians Paul wrote, "Put into practice what you have learned and received from me, both from my words and from my deeds. And the God who gives us peace will be with you" (Phil. 4:9 TEV). But most of us cannot be quite that confident in our own Christian lives.

What is the solution? Who could you imitate? Is there anyone who could be a pattern for your life? By all means, there is a pattern for life. But go to the source. Don't be satisfied with imitations. Refuse to accept anything less than the best. Jesus Christ is the pattern for our lives.

From Jesus Christ we can learn the true meaning of reliance on God, communion with the Father, compassion toward others, and self-giving, self-sacrificing love.

Look at your spiritual life. Is it an imitation? or is it real?

Look at the pattern for your life. Is it an imitation of an imitation? Or is it patterned after the real thing—Christ?

Don't be an imitation of an imitation. Let Christ be your guide. Seek to pattern your life after Him. Let Him fill your life.

preparation: a key to success

General Douglas MacArthur's father, Arthur MacArthur, was also a military officer. Therefore Douglas MacArthur spent his growing-up years at various military bases. He did not have the opportunity of sustained schooling for his high school education. When he got ready to take the competitive examinations for appointment to West Point, he went to Milwaukee and entered high school. He also established a rigid study schedule to prepare for the exams.

In his autobiography, *Reminiscences,* he said: "When the marks were counted, I led. My careful preparation had repaid me. It was a lesson I never forgot. Preparedness is the key to success and victory."[1]

That is a good lesson: Preparedness is the key to success and victory.

This is as true in the Lord's work as it is for examinations, military affairs, or athletic endeavors.

Consider the Sunday school teacher who does not prepare the lesson. What could have been an exciting adventure in Biblical learning becomes instead a dull hour that passes very slowly.

More committee meetings could have been made to

[1]Douglas MacArthur, *Reminiscences.* (New York: McGraw-Hill Book Company, 1964), p. 18.

be meaningful experiences of Christian service if only the chairman had taken time for adequate preparation. Instead the meetings were sad and frustrating experiences of humans grappling with their own problems as well as the ones they were attempting to solve.

And what about the countless sermons that could have been memorable if only they had been well prepared?

Time is valuable. The person who leads as well as the person who follows or attends or listens has little time to waste. Lack of adequate preparation is a waste of time for all concerned.

Do you want to be more successful in your church work? Then take MacArthur's lesson to heart: Preparedness is the key to success and victory.

people pollute

After the water level of Cane River Lake was lowered to allow the city to construct protective walls along the river bank, the boys and I cleaned out the river behind our house one Saturday morning. We were knee deep in mud and water, and Chyrisse supervised from the shore. You can hardly imagine what we got out of the river! We found beer bottles and cans by the score, old soft drink bottles, whiskey and wine bottles, a wagon wheel, and cans of every description, including a garbage can.

At one point while we were struggling to get everything cleaned out along a stretch of the bank, Chyrisse observed, "Daddy, people sure pollute our river, don't they?"

Well, they do. But actually she could have left off a part of her statement and still be correct. It would have been just as true to have said, "People pollute."

In the current ecological interest we have heard this many times. People pollute our environment. We have adopted what Helmut Thielicke once described as "the master of the house" attitude. God has give us a world to use, but we have abused it. We have considered ourselves to be masters when really we are servants.

People pollute the moral environment, too. Many people are upset at the permissive direction in which society is moving. Plays, movies, and books seem to get more explicit sexually as time goes on. Lack of concern over moral issues is frightening. Hate and deviousness are often not even considered as moral issues. People have polluted our moral as well as our physical environment.

And people pollute their own lives. It is absolutely amazing to see the fixes into which some people get their lives. The old word for it is *sin*. It is still applicable.

People pollute. But God cleanses. God will cleanse. God can cleanse and change any life given to Him in faith. Why not try it?

do you know where your children are?

Have you ever noticed the little public service announcement carried by many local TV stations? It states, "It is 10 (or 11) o'clock. Do you know where your children are?"

That is a good question. Periodically, each parent should stop and ask himself the same question, "Do I know where my children are?"

The most obvious application is, "Do you know where your children are physically?" That is the intent of the TV question. Who are they with? Where are they? What are they doing? Consider the amount of agony, hurt, and heartaches that could be averted simply by parents responsibly answering this question. Companions and places of recreation have a lot to do with shaping the character and outlook of our children.

You should also ask, "Do I know where our children are intellectually?" What are they thinking? Are they thinking? Who is shaping their ideas? Most of us as parents don't take enough time to talk with our children to have much idea of what they are thinking. Parents sometimes are shocked when their children come up with some weird ideas. They could have helped in the shaping of those ideas if they had just taken the time and the interest to do it.

A very important question is, "Do you know where your children are spiritually?" The spiritual development of young people is extremely important. Proper spiritual development will not happen just by chance any more than good health or good intellectual development will happen by chance. Have you heard of any parents keeping their children out of school because they were afraid that they would turn their children against school by insisting that they attend? But how often we have heard this statement about church! Spiritual development is a parent's responsibility. No one else can guide a child spiritually as effectively as a parent.

Do you know where your children are? If not, you probably will want to check on it.

of tires, troubles, and triumphs

One day a preacher went down to the store with three bicycle tires, all from different bicycles, to be repaired. Only a week or so before that he had to buy a full set of automobile tires. And it had not been too long before that when he had to get a set of tires for the other car. He had experienced some real tire problems.

When the service man came back with the three tires repaired, he said, "Preacher, I just don't understand this. If you had been Mr._____ [and he called the name of a well-known liquor dealer] I could understand it better. But I just don't understand why you are having so much trouble."

Everyone laughed at that, of course. But he was expressing something that a lot of people think: somehow Christians should be immune to trouble; somehow God should protect those who serve Him.

After the San Francisco earthquake and the fire that followed had reduced the city to shambles, a newspaper reporter noticed a liquor distillery standing intact in the devastation. He wrote:

> If, as they say, God spanked this town
> For being over-frisky
> Why did he burn the churches down
> and spare Old Hopalong's whisky?

This has been a problem for Christians as long as there has been Christianity. Experience shows us that Christians experience troubles, illnesses, heartbreak, and problems just as all other people do.

If God does not have some special wall of protection around the believer, what does He do? I'll tell you what God does. God gives the Christian a vision that looks beyond the immediate problem. God gives the Christian a source of strength in the middle of the difficulty. God gives the Christian an assurance that he has a faith that can withstand any blow of circumstance.

No, God does not give Christians an immunity to trouble. But God does give us a faith, a strength, and a power to face life and its problems because we live with the Lord of life.

watching the other fellow's cork

Craig and Keith and their Dad went fishing on Toledo Bend Lake during a July 4th holiday. They were trying to catch some of those fine bluegill bream that hang out over there.

They were all three sitting in the boat without a bite. Suddenly Dad noticed that Keith's cork was about a foot under water. He yelled for him to pull in his fish. About that time Craig's cork disappeared beneath the surface. But he had been watching his Dad's cork.

As it turned out, each one was watching the other fellow's cork. Dad was watching Keith's cork; Keith was watching Craig's; and Craig was watching Dad's. Nobody was minding his own business. And as a consequence, no one caught a fish.

Most of us spend too much time watching the other fellow's cork. We know exactly how the neighbor family ought to raise their children; we know precisely the decision our friend should make; we know exactly why our acquaintance's business didn't work out. There is no doubt about it; if we were given the opportunity of running the other fellow's affairs, things would work out much differently.

But we are not given that opportunity. Frankly, we have trouble enough managing our own affairs. We do not know the background out of which our friend or neighbor makes his decisions. We don't know the ramifications of a certain course of action.

What we actually are saying is, "If I were doing that, I would do it differently." Differently, yes. But probably not better.

The Bible tells us to bear one another's burdens, not to add to their burdens. One way we add to the burdens of others is by minding their business, guessing their motives, and passing our judgments upon their actions along to others.

You catch a lot more fish when you watch your own cork.

"we make people happy"

Did you ever have the privilege of visiting Astroworld and watching the people who work there? It seems that every Astroworld employee has one on. They are little round orange buttons with the words "We Make People Happy" printed on them.

That's what they say: "We Make People Happy." But they really don't. They may give an opportunity for fun. They may provide pleasure. They may enable people to be entertained. They may set up diversions. But they don't make people happy.

I saw some people there who didn't look happy. I saw people standing in endless lines with very bored expressions on their faces. They weren't happy. I saw a father with some children, and I could imagine that they were on his twice-a-month visitation weekend. They laughed once, but they weren't happy. I saw a woman with an arrogant look who fussed at her husband in front of their children, disdainfully called him "Your majesty" and dispatched him on an errand. They later smiled at a clown, but they weren't happy. I saw some people who showed by their dress and their manner that they could hardly afford their visit to Astroworld. Possibly, as they thought of how many hours of work it took to provide the tickets or how many groceries that same money would buy even at today's inflated prices, they weren't happy. I saw an exhausted child take on another ride forced by a parent determined that the child would "enjoy" himself. He hollered in excitement when he "lost his stomach," but he wasn't happy.

When will we ever learn? Happiness is neither mechanically nor externally produced. Entertainment, pleasure, diversions, and even fun do not produce happiness.

Happiness is internal. It comes about when we are rightly related to God and can find satisfaction and contentment no matter what goes on around us.

I think it was Thomas Carlyle who said: "Not all the financiers, upholsters and confectioners joined together in a stock company can make one shoe-black happy for more than an hour or so, because the shoe-black has an immortal soul in him quite other than his stomach, which would require the infinite universe to fulfill."

Who makes people happy? Only God makes people happy.

doing what comes naturally . . . and getting hurt by it

Our little bob-tailed fox terrier, Punkin, is no different from any other dog. When a cat comes in the yard he begins to bristle. Then he will chase it out of the yard. As far as dogs are concerned, this is doing what comes naturally.

But, you know, one can get hurt by just doing what comes naturally. Just recently, a big tom cat ventured into our yard. Punkin saw him, and then took off in pursuit. The cat started running. It looked as though Punkin would chase the cat out of the yard and that would be it. But at about half-way across the yard, the cat stopped, turned on Punkin and tore into him. And the feline really tore him up! With one slash of a paw he laid open Punkin's right shoulder. The cut was about three inches long, through the skin, and into the flesh. Now, poor Punkin had been doing only what came naturally for a dog to do, but he got hurt by it.

A lot of what people do today is dismissed as simply doing what comes naturally. But a lot of people are hurt by it.

The Bible talks about sin. However, there are always folks who dismiss the reality of sin. They say that the failures, the wrongs, the hurts that are caused to others, and the lies 'and untruths are just doing what comes naturally. But think how many people are hurt by these actions.

We hear it a lot these days, in discussions about sex particularly. We see around us the deteriorating family life and the looser views toward sexual morality, and someone is always nearby to say that it is just doing what comes naturally. They will say that it is unnatural for one man and one woman to commit themselves to one another for life. They will say that it is frustrating for young people not to express their desires fully. But look at the number of people hurt by it: illegitimate children, a rising VD rate, broken homes, guilt-ridden people, and greater frustration.

Doing what comes naturally is the world's explanation for many activities that Christians call sin. But watch out, you can be hurt by it.

the number one problem in the United States

A little girl of about six or seven said to her mother, "The number one problem in the United States is pollution. I read that in my *Weekly Reader*. Everybody knows that the number one problem in the United States is pollution, everybody but our preacher. He thinks it is sin. But I guess that's just because he's a preacher."

Actually, the preacher may not be too far wrong. Even pollution can be a result of sin. We refuse to treat God's good earth with respect. To subdue the earth does not mean to destroy the earth.

Sin takes many forms. It may show up in selfishness or in self-abuse or in self-centeredness. It can be individual or social.

Sin has its effects socially. Many of the problems that confront us now have grown out of the results of our rebelliousness and refusal to follow the will of God. Many people face difficult problems, disturbed lives, and generally messed-up situations either because of their sin or the sin of someone close to them.

As the Bible states it: "For all have sinned and come short of the glory of God." As long as this is true—and it still is—sin will continue to be the number one problem in the United States.

Maybe if people other than preachers thought that, we could begin to do something about it.

part ten

ABOUT CHRISTIAN CELEBRATIONS

something new just for me

Bishop Gerald Kennedy of the Methodist Church tells about a boy who received a new coat through a social worker. She noticed him examining it very carefully. When she asked him if anything was wrong, he replied that there was nothing and then said, "Thank God for something new." It may have been the first time in his whole life he had ever received any clothing that was new. Probably everything else he ever had was "previously owned." This was something new just for him.

The New Year before us gives each of us something new—and it is just for you.

A new year is a new opportunity. Those things that we have been wanting to do "sometime" we can to do now. This year will give us a new opportunity for this.

If you had planned to begin practicing stewardship, this new year will be a new opportunity for you.

If you had hoped to begin a practicing ministry as a Christian, this new year will be a new opportunity for you.

If you had meant to start Christian witnessing, this new year will be a new opportunity for you.

If you had planned to make some changes in your personality, this new year will be a new opportunity.

If you had wanted to get around to being a better parent, this new year will be a new opportunity for you.

The new year provides something new just for you. Each of us has a year either to invest wisely or to spend foolishly. And the choice is up to you.

I don't know about you, but I am glad for this new year. I hope to use it well, and I hope you will, too.

getting the illustration . . .
and missing the point

During the week before Easter, a pastor had the privilege of talking to a first-grade class in a public school about the meaning of Easter. In trying to illustrate the tomb in which Jesus was laid, he drew a little picture on the blackboard. After finishing the presentation he asked if any of the children had any questions. Immediately a hand shot up. Then one boy informed the pastor that he had not drawn the stone big enough because it didn't completely cover the entrance to the tomb. He got the illustration, but he had missed the point.

Many of us do that on Easter. We get involved in the popular illustrations of new life—baby chicks, Easter eggs, the first buds of spring, breaking out the spring clothes—but we miss what Easter teaches us about new life in Christ.

We can give all the details of the Easter story, including the size of the stone that covered the entrance to the tomb, but we miss the greatest fact—how Christ is to live in the heart of every believer.

The Easter message is central to the Christian faith. The one who gave Himself for us in self-sacrifice is now alive! He lives in the heart of each Christian. He gives new life to old lives when they are given to Him in faith and commitment. He intercedes for us. He guides us. His power and presence are present realities.

This Easter, let's get the whole story. Let's not be guilty of getting the illustration, but missing the point.

another theory blown

Mike Murphy and his friend sneaked off to Toledo Bend Lake for an afternoon of fishing. The closer they got to the lake the more threatening the clouds became. They discussed the theory that they had both heard many times before: If you fish just before a weather change, the fish will bite like mad.

They had an opportunity to put that theory to the test. They had been fishing only about an hour when suddenly the weather changed. The sky grew dark. The clouds converged. The wind blew. And the rain came. They went to shore and sought shelter in a small grove of pine trees. While they were standing under the trees munching apples and trying to keep from getting water-logged, his friend reminded Mike of the theory they had discussed earlier. His reply was, "Yeah. We just blew another theory."

When Jesus Christ was resurrected from the dead He blew a theory to bits. The theory was that once a man was dead he was finished. But Jesus showed that He was not finished. He conquered death, sin, and Satan. He arose from the dead!

The enemies of Jesus had a neat little theory. They had the final solution to the Jesus problem. They would put Him to death. No longer would they be bothered by Him.

But on the third day, on that first Easter morning, Jesus blew their theory. By rising from the grave Jesus showed forever that life was stronger than death, that love was stronger than hate, that God was stronger than sin. Jesus arose from the dead and lives forevermore!

We sometimes blow somebody's pet theory. What they know to be true may sometimes prove false. If nothing else, Easter shows us another theory blown. The power of God cannot be stopped—not by men, death, or the grave.

the surprise of Easter

They really did not expect to find that tomb empty on that first Easter morning. When the disciples of Jesus laid Him in the new tomb of Joseph of Arimathea, they had no idea that His body would not be there when they returned. In fact, you will remember, on the way to the tomb the women discussed the task of rolling away the stone from the door. Knowing the end of the story, it is hard for us to realistically estimate the real surprise of Easter.

But the surprise of Easter has not ended. With the coming of each Easter season, we are reminded again of some significant surprises.

Some people are surprised that love can overcome hate. These people live their lives in such a state of hate, malice, ill will, and confusion that they are genuinely surprised that love can overcome hate. Hate is not the last word—and Easter proves it.

Some people are surprised that suffering can be redemptive. Suffering for so many has been embittering, callousing, and limiting. But Easter shows us that the suffering of Christ was the price of our redemption.

Some people are surprised that life can overcome death. With a pessimistic view of life and human nature, many seem convinced that death is the end. Easter assures us that life is stronger than death.

These are Easter surprises. And these comprise the heart of the Easter faith—a faith in the resurrected Christ.

"the lady what cooks"

I wonder what "Women's Lib" is going to do to Mother's Day! One of the most significant features about Mother's Day is the recognition that mothers are uniquely special. Mothers occupy a particular place in the lives of most people. They have something that makes them distinctive.

There is an interesting passage in Alice Lee Humphries's delightful little book based on her teaching experiences, *Heaven in My Hand*. She was visiting in the home of Pamela, one of her students. The family was very poor. Pamela began in a straightforward way to point out some of the evidences of their poverty as reflected in the furniture, the wallpaper, and the leaks in the roof.

In the course of this conversation, the pleasant odors from the kitchen began to waft into the room and a glimpse was seen of Pamela's mother preparing the meal. Hoping to change the subject, which had become somewhat embarassing to her, the teacher remarked to Pamela that her mother must be a wonderful cook. "My mother is no cook," Pamela declared in her low, clear voice, "she is *the lady* what cooks."

Now this puts things into perspective. A mother often gets the feeling that her family considers her to be nothing but a cook, a housekeeper, a washwoman, a taskmaster, or a taxicab driver. But never confuse the function with the person. While a mother may perform all these and a hundred or so more tasks for her family, she is never just a cook or a housekeeper or a washwoman or a taskmaster or a taxicab driver. She is always "*the lady* what does those things." She has value and worth and dignity as a person. Her task or function at that time is simply what she may be doing out of her commitment and love for her family.

"The lady what cooks." On this Mother's Day, remember to make the distinctions you need to make. Don't confuse the person with her function.

responsible . . . for what?

In the Hebrew home, the father had a real responsibility. Besides being the head of the house, he was also responsible for family worship. He represented God to his family.

Did you ever wonder why Jesus chose the word *father* to express our relationship to God? God is not an indulgent uncle. God is not a doting grandfather. Nor is God an approving friend. God is our Father.

God is represented as our Father because the characteristics of God's dealing with us are similar to those of a good human father. God loves us. But He is also interested in our discipline, our development, and our character. A father is benevolent but not indulgent, gentle but not unprincipled.

It is said that ministers in some deprived areas are not able to present God as Father. The only father that some of these children know is one who mistreated them, deprived them, deserted them, or generally made life miserable for them. This is not the correct picture of God.

What kind of responsibility does this give to Christian fathers? If a father represents God to his family, and father is the concept Jesus used to describe our relationship to God, then every father has a tremendous responsibility. He has a responsibility for guiding his family in worship and in the discovery of God. He has a responsibility for showing God's love. He has a responsibility for reminding his family of God's relationship to them.

Responsible . . . for what? The father is responsible for Christian life and development. On this Father's Day, let's take a giant step in this direction.

practicing our profession

As we get close to Father's Day, I have thought some about my father. My father was a fine man with a distinctive Christian witness.

We moved to Shreveport in 1937 from Arkansas. At that time he opened and managed a feed store. Although it was not until a good many years later that he became a partner in the business, he was the manager of the Feeder's Supply Company until the day of his death.

At one time he received an opportunity to become manager of another feed store that was located at the other end of the building in which Feeder's Supply was located. The offer included a considerable increase in salary.

After he had made his decision not to take the new offer, I asked him why he had decided not to work with the other company. He said, "Well, son, all these years I have been telling these people that Purina feed was the best for their livestock. If I started telling them something else now, it would seem that I had been lying all this time."

That is integrity. He practiced what he professed to believe.

We don't always act like that, do we? As it has often been said, we talk a better ball game than we play. And we do this as Christians, too.

We may talk about our concern for others, but when it comes to witnessing or other acts of real caring we must admit that we have not been that concerned.

We may talk about the joy that comes into life from being a Christian, but it may be hard to find any evidences of joy in our life.

We may say that we are practicing Biblical stewardship, but we fail to give much of our money for God's ministry through the church.

There are many ways in which we are guilty of making people think that we were not really committed to what we had been professing. But there is one way of showing that we are committed to what we have professed. And that is to make our lives consistent with our confession at all points. With God's help we can do that.

what does liberty mean to you?

A couple was planning their marriage for the Fourth of July weekend. On the night of the wedding rehearsal, as preparations were being made to get the rehearsal underway, someone happened to look up at the front of the church auditorium and spotted a sign that had been hung above the baptistry and choir loft. It was a sign to be used in connection with a Fourth of July building-fund drive, and in large letters it read, "Liberty: What does it mean to you?"

Maybe this is an appropriate question to ask at a wedding. Surely it is an appropriate question to ask Christians on the Fourth of July.

What does liberty mean to you? Does it mean license? Does it mean undisciplined freedom to do anything you want? Is it understood just in terms of personal rights with no regard for others?

Christian liberty should always take into consideration other people, discipline, privileges, and responsibility.

The most liberating force in the world is the liberty that the Christian finds in Jesus Christ. It liberates from the fear of sin, self, Satan, and tomorrow. It lifts life higher than the level of selfish concern for prestige, power, and position.

It is an absolutely mistaken concept of the Christian faith to think of it as a restricting force. Instead, there is a liberating quality that gives meaning to all of life. Through Christ the believer is free to be what God can enable him to be and intends for him to be.

Paul was the one who said it: "Freedom is what we have—Christ has set us free! Stand, then, as free men, and do not allow yourselves to become slaves again" (Gal. 5:1 TEV).

It is a good question to put before Christians and citizens any time. But especially is it significant as we approach Independence Day. Answer it for yourself. "Liberty: What does it mean to me?"

a tribute to some radical nonconformists

They were actually radical nonconformists who did not think very highly of the "Establishment." If fact, they were so upset with the "Establishment" that they moved many miles to a wilderness area and set up an experimental community.

Things didn't go too well at first in their experimental community. There was some violence. Some of the people had to learn how to live together. It looked as though they might have some opposition from their nearest neighbors. Because of outbreaks of disease and other hardships many of them died. When they did make friends with their neighbors they were not people of whom many of their old friends would approve.

But they made a go of it in this experimental community. After a year or so they were so pleased with the social changes they had brought about that they decided to celebrate. They invited their new friends, ceased all work, and threw a big party.

Who were these radical nonconformists? We call them Pilgrims. Their big party was the first Thanksgiving in America. And after three hundred and fifty years, we still pay tribute to these people.

In our efforts to keep things on an even keel, we often forget our own beginnings. Both as Christians and as Americans, we began as nonconformists—as revolutionaries, as rockers-of-the-boat. From this heritage we have a strong legacy of independence, innovation, and ability to meet new situations creatively.

At this Thanksgiving season, we pay tribute to these radical nonconformists. May we still retain enough of their spirit to live creatively in our new day.

no room where?

The saddest statement in the Christmas story is, "There was no room for them in the inn." For the very Creator of the world, there was no room in the inn. The world was little prepared for the coming of Christ.

The world is little prepared today for the coming of Christ. We do not shut Him out of the inn and shove Him into a stable. But we crowd Him out of a place much more significant—our lives.

There may be no room for Christ because we have restricted His influence to an increasingly smaller corner of our life. Other interests, other demands, other allegiances take precedence over the One who gave us new life.

We can be so rushed at the Christmas season that no room is left for the Master. An endless round of parties and dinners, countless presents to be bought, plans for the holidays . . . and suddenly Christmas is here, and we discover that we have completely shut Christ out of our Christmas.

Commerce sometimes pushes Christ out of our lives. If Christmas is viewed solely in commercial terms, we can have little room for the One who gave His life, the greatest gift, for us.

"No room in the inn." No room where? Could it be there is no room in your heart for Christ at Christmas?

merry Christmas!

It is that time of year again. We conclude our telephone conversations with a "Merry Christmas!" We say "Merry Christmas" instead of "Good-bye" when we leave friends. We sign our correspondence "Merry Christmas."